ro
ro
ro

rororo

rororo sprachen

Herausgegeben von Ludwig Moos

Das schlechte Gewissen meldet sich immer mal wieder: Man müsste mehr für seine Sprachkenntnisse tun. Aber da dies Zeit und Mühe kostet, bleibt es meist beim guten Vorsatz. Dieses Sprachbuch lockt Büffelmuffel mit Witz und didaktischer Raffinesse aus der Reserve und zeigt, dass Sprachenlernen kein Privileg der Emsigen oder Begabten sein muss. Eine amüsante Geschichte, die fortlaufend zu lesen ist, macht vertraut mit dem englischen Alltag und den Sprechmitteln zu seiner Bewältigung. Ein Schwerpunkt pro Doppelseite bringt das notwendige Minimum an Wissen auf den Punkt, lockere Tests helfen dabei, das frisch Gelernte einzuüben und zu behalten.

René Bosewitz · Robert Kleinschroth

Englisch für Büffelmuffel

Rowohlt Taschenbuch Verlag

7. Auflage Februar 2008

Originalausgabe
Veröffentlicht im Rowohlt Taschenbuch Verlag,
Reinbek bei Hamburg, September 2004

Umschlaggestaltung Britta Lemke
(Illustration Britta Lemke)
Layout Anne Drude
Satz OCR-A und Stone, PostScript Linotype Library, QuarkXPress 3.31
Gesamtherstellung Clausen & Bosse, Leck
Printed in Germany
ISBN 978 3 499 61907 6

CONTENT

INHALT

Willkommen im Club der Büffelmuffel! Eigentlich ist Ihr Englisch ganz passabel – aber nur „eigentlich". Haben Sie vielleicht länger pausiert und vieles schon vergessen? Sie möchten also wieder einsteigen, wollen aber auch nicht bei Null anfangen. Da sind Sie hier goldrichtig, denn das Buch ist für alle gemacht, die keine Lust zum Pauken und Büffeln haben, aber auf vergnügliche Weise trotzdem etwas lernen wollen. Wie soll das gehen?

Sie haben ein spannendes mit Humor gewürztes Lese- und Lernbuch aufgeschlagen, das ein wenig Schulenglisch voraussetzt. Es unterscheidet sich grundsätzlich von den üblichen Lehrbüchern durch Form und Inhalt. Es ist für alle jene geschrieben, die nicht die Zeit oder die Ausdauer haben, sich durch ein konventionelles Lehrwerk zu kämpfen.

Im Grunde wollen wir ja alle etwas lernen oder wenigstens Gelerntes bewahren. Wenn es nur nicht so mühsam wäre! Deshalb haben wir für Sie eine unterhaltsame Geschichte geschrieben, die Sie zum Lesen und Lernen verleiten wird. Dazu brauchen Sie pro Kapitel etwa 10 bis 30 Minuten, je nachdem welcher Gattung Büffelmuffel Sie angehören.

Und nach jeder Episode werden Sie das Buch nicht erschöpft weglegen, sondern wissen wollen, wie es weitergeht. Das sollen Sie auch – selbst unterwegs, im Zug oder in Wartezimmern.

1. Sind Sie ein *eiliger* Büffelmuffel? Dann folgen Sie der Geschichte in den oberen Seitenhälften. Sie lesen sich ein und erschließen schon bald unbekannten Wortschatz aus dem Zusammenhang. Wenn Sie mal hängen bleiben, genügt ein Blick zu den Worterklärungen am Seitenrand, und Sie verstehen alles. Vielleicht haben Sie auch noch Zeit für den einen oder anderen Witz.
2. Sind Sie ein *nicht so eiliger* Büffelmuffel, entnehmen Sie dem Blickpunkt, wo wir die Schwerpunkte gesetzt haben. Sie lesen den Text und wählen anschließend die Tests aus, die es Ihnen wert erscheinen. Sie sind kurz und abwechslungsreich. Die Lösungen finden Sie im Anhang.
3. Dem *gründlicheren* Büffelmuffel brauchen wir nicht zu sagen, was zu tun ist. Sie werden das Kapitel lesen, vielleicht auch noch ein zweites Mal und anschließend die zugehörigen Tests machen. Sie werden sich vielleicht auch die Zeit nehmen, die Erläuterungen im Schlüssel zu lesen.

Noch ein paar Lerntipps auf den Weg:
Die Wortschatzspalte rechts vom Text hat zwei Funktionen. Sie dient zuerst dem Textverständnis. Sie brauchen kein Wort nachzuschlagen, sondern können flüssig weiterlesen. Im Anschluss an die Lektüre eines Kapitels sollten alle Büffelmuffel die schräg gedruckten Ausdrücke im Text überfliegen und sich an die Übersetzung erinnern.
Der gründlichere Büffelmuffel wird außerdem die deutsche Spalte senkrecht lesen und sich den nebenstehenden englischen Ausdruck ins Gedächtnis rufen. Ein Blick zur Kontrolle auf das Schräggedruckte im Text, und der Zusammenhang ist wieder da. Dies ist eine sinnvolle und nachhaltige Form des Wortschatzlernens und trainiert Ihr Gedächtnis. Den gesamten Wortschatz und eine komplette Liste der unregelmäßigen Verben finden Sie alphabetisch geordnet im Anhang. Apropos Anhang, testen Sie doch zum Abschluss Ihre Grammatikfestigkeit anhand unseres *Grammar Check*. Da die Tests den Schwerpunkten der Kapitel folgen, können Sie dies auch nach jedem Kapitel tun. Wir wünschen Ihnen angenehme Unterhaltung und frohes Schaffen.

Robert Kleinschroth und René Bosewitz

1 how it all began

Once upon a time there was a lovely old *mansion* in the south of England. A rich gentleman, Sir Arthur Blair, *built* it in the eighteenth century. It had at least twelve bedrooms.	*Es war einmal; Her renhaus* *bauen*
One day a certain Mr Swindler who *had come into* some *money bought* the mansion. His aunt had quietly *passed away* some weeks earlier.	*zu Geld kommen* *kaufen* *versterben*
This highly motivated but *tricky* gentleman *turned* the mansion into a small country hotel, *although* he was anything else but a professional hotel manager. You'll find out about that yourselves, though.	*schlau; verwandeln* *obwohl*

Auf einen BLICK

	Schwerpunkt	Beispiel
1.	Past Tense	Mr Swindler *bought* the mansion
2.	Past Perfect	He *had come* into some money.

TEST 1: Beherrschen Sie die Vorvergangenheit

Für das Satzgefüge gilt: Erzählt man Ereignisse in der Vergangenheit (*Past Tense*), stehen Ereignisse, *die davor passierten*, in der Vorvergangenheit (*Past Perfect*).

Verbinden Sie die Sätze zu einem Satz
A. mit dem Relativpronomen *who* und / oder **B.** mit *after.*

1. His aunt had passed away. Mr Swindler came into some money. (*after*)
2. Mr Swindler came into some money. He bought the mansion. (*who / after*)
3. His aunt passed away on the 30th of August. She had been a teacher for 30 years.

The *"would-be" hotel* was part of the town of Hastings in the old English county of East Sussex and *looked out* across the beach and sea *to* France. Mr Ronald Swindler, Ron for short, *converted* the bedrooms to small apartments, installed kitchens in the *cellars* and lounges near to the *reception*. And so the hotel, the Holiday Out, *was born*.
Swindler had some very *strange* ideas as to what the guest of a typical country hotel should be like and what services a country hotel should *offer*: "No TV in the bedrooms. Too many people are brainwashed by the *box*." Our story *takes place* in and around this palace of *relaxation* as we meet the characters who have the *misfortune* to become guests of Mr Swindler's "paradise".

Möchtegern-Hotel
Blick haben auf
umbauen
Keller
Empfang
war geboren
sonderbar
anbieten
Flimmerkiste
stattfinden; Entspannung; Unglück

TEST 2: Mit anderen Worten

Ron *got* some money.	Ron ________ some money.
His aunt *died* quietly.	His aunt quietly ________.
He *changed* the rooms to apartments.	He ________ them to apartments.

TEST 3: Richtig (R) oder falsch (F)

R F

1. The mansion had at least twelve bedrooms.
2. The mansion was built in the nineteenth century.
3. Mr Swindler got it from his aunt.
4. The kitchens are in the cellar.

TEST 4: Übersetzen Sie

Übersetzungshilfen

answer, ask, cash, receptionist, traveller's checks, walk

Ein Mann geht in ein Hotel und fragt: „Nehmen Sie Kinder?" Der Herr am Empfang antwortet: „Nein, nur Bargeld und Reiseschecks."

2 2 planning the holiday

Our *adventure* begins back in old Germany where a loving couple, young and naïve, and very *eager* to *spend* some of their time in romantic England, are preparing for their journey. Heidi Schmelz (**H**) and Bernd Bubel (**B**).

H: Come on! *Get a move on*, or we'll never *decide* where we want to go.
B: Heidi, *leave me alone.* You're always rushing. People who *rush* make mistakes.
H: Bernd, you know very well that I don't make mistakes. Now, let's *spread* this map out and fix our *destination.* Here we are, South East England.
B: Look at this travel brochure and this lovely old hotel. It's not *expensive.* Just let me *convert* the price into euros so we can *compare.*
H: I've done it already. It's sixty euros a night for *half board.* And if we stay a whole week we get it even *cheaper.*

Abenteuer
begierig
verbringen
Mach schon; beschließen
lass mich in Ruhe
überstürzen
ausbreiten
Reiseziel
teuer; umrechnen
vergleichen
Halbpension
billiger

Auf einen BLICK: Der Imperativ[1]

	Schwerpunkt	Beispiel
1.	Anweisung: Verb im Infinitiv[2]	*Come* on! Get a move on.
2.	Verbot: *Don't* vor dem Infinitiv	*Don't keep* talking.

Daneben finden Sie folgende Formen der Anweisung im Text:

1. And *do* hurry! Vorangestelltes *Do* verstärkt die Anweisung.
2. *You* phone the hotel and I'll contact the ferry company. Vorangestelltes *You* ist emotional, umgangssprachlich.
3. *Let's* spread this map out. Mit *Let us* bezieht man sich in einen Vorschlag mit ein.

1 *Imperativ* ist die Befehlsform 2 *Infinitiv* ist die Grundform des Verbs

B: Our holidays start on August 1st, so we still have *plenty of time.*

H: Don't keep talking about time. Now, what about the trip? I think we should *travel* by car. It will make us more flexible.

B: Listen, Heidi, I'm not so sure. It's very *expensive* to cross the Channel. And it's difficult to use a *left-hand drive* car in England. Let's rent a car over there. I read that you can get one *cheaply* if you do it in a small town.

H: Perhaps you're right. Okay, we'll use this little town of Hastings as a *base* and make tours from there. You phone the hotel and I'll contact the ferry company. And do *hurry*!

viel Zeit
reisen
teuer
Linkssteuerung
billig
Ausgangspunkt
sich beeilen

TEST 1: Meistern Sie den Imperativ

Do, Don't oder *Don't you*?

1. "__________ *worry*[1]," a patient told his psychiatrist. "I'll pay every penny I owe[2], or my name isn't Alexander the Great!"
2. Patient: Shall I start at the beginning?
   Doctor: __________, please.
   Patient: Well, in the beginning I created Heaven and Earth.
3. Tom: __________ *pull* faces[3] at my parrot[4]! He's very sensitive[5].
   Bob: All right, but he started it!

TEST 2: Probleme mit den kleinen Wörtern?

1. Heidi and Bernd are eager to spend some time in England.
2. Their holidays start on August 1st.
3. They are preparing for their journey.
4. They look at a travel brochure.
5. They will travel by car.
6. They get a move on.

1 sich Sorgen machen 2 schulden 3 Gesichter schneiden 4 Papagei 5 empfindlich

	Bernd telephones Holiday Out to *make the booking*. Bernd (**B**), Ron Swindler (**R**).	*buchen*
R:	Swindler *speaking*. It's only a name. What can I do for you?	*am Apparat*
B:	Excuse me, could I speak to *reception*, please?	*Empfang*
S:	Reception? Yes, that's me. Reception, cook, *chamber maid*, gardener, owner. You name it, I do it. You can't get good *staff* nowadays, and if you get them, they're always on holiday.	*Zimmermädchen* *Personal*
B:	Oh! Actually I'm phoning to book a room for two people for the summer.	
R:	Yes, that's what they all want. Rooms for the summer. And then the summer doesn't arrive and it rains. Then they all begin to *complain* ... to *me*! Actually I don't have a *direct line* to *heaven*. I can't change it. What dates?	*sich beschweren* *heißer Draht* *Himmel*

TEST 3: Englisch am Telefon – Was fehlt hier?

Guten Tag. Was kann ich für Sie tun?	Good morning. What _____ I do _______ you?
Darf ich nach dem Grund Ihres Anrufs fragen?	Could I ________ the purpose of your ___________?
Es geht um Ihre Annonce.	It's _______ your advert.
Ich rufe an, um ein Zimmer zu reservieren.	I'm __________ to _______ a room.

TEST 4: Word Power – Was ist gemeint?

1. Place where you plan to arrive at	*d* _ _ _ _ _ _ _ _ _ _
2. There they deal with people who arrive	*r* _ _ _ _ _ _ _ _
3. Say that you are not happy	*c* _ _ _ _ _ _ _
4. The hotel belongs to him	*o* _ _ _ _

R:	What dates?	
B:	Oh, August 1st for *at least* a week.	*wenigstens*
R:	People?	
B:	Yes, *of course.*	*natürlich*
R:	No, I realise you are people. How many?	
B:	There are two of us.	
R:	Sex?	*Geschlecht*
B:	Well, sometimes, but...	
R:	No, I mean *gender* of the guests.	*Geschlecht*
B:	*Male* and *female.*	*männlich; weiblich; annehmen*
R:	Aha! Not married, I *suppose*. Well, it's not my business, and I don't care if you're not. Now, you have to pay a *deposit* by credit card. What's your card and your number?	*Anzahlung*

TEST 5: Idiomatisches Englisch – Erinnern Sie sich?

Ersetzen Sie das Unsinnswort *woggle.*

1. Get a *woggle* on.	*m*__________
2. You're always *woggling.*	*r*__________
3. *Woggle* me alone.	*l*__________
4. It's not my *woggle.*	*b*__________

TEST 6: Haben Sie verstanden? Richtig (R) oder falsch (F)?

	R	F
1. One night at the Holiday-Out hotel is €60.		
2. They will have to pay in advance.		
3. Our couple's holiday starts on August 1st.		
4. They will travel in their own car.		
5. Mr Swindler has a gardener and a chamber maid.		

3 teething troubles[1]

Bernd and Heidi arrive at Stansted Airport. The ever careful Bernd had *got a bargain*. He had booked seats on Ruin Airways, one euro a seat.	*ein gutes Geschäft machen*
At the airport:	
B: Well, that was a *pleasant* journey. We had no turbulence and it only *lasted* fifty-five minutes. Look, it's *only* eleven o'clock.	*angenehm* *dauern* *erst*
H: Bernd, you always buy the *cheapest* of everything. It's almost the middle of the night and we don't even know if there's a train to Hastings at this time. Quick, *get a move* on. Let's ask at the *information desk*.	*das Billigste* *beeile dich; Auskunft*
At the information desk: Clerk (C)	
C: And how can I help you, Sir?	
B: We've just arrived from Germany. We'd like to get to Hastings.	
C: I'm afraid the next train *departs* tomorrow morning at 8:15.	*abfahren*
H: I just knew it. Now we*'re* really *in the soup*. It's your *fault*.	*in der Tinte sitzen* *Schuld*
B: Miss, what does a taxi to Hastings *cost*?	*kosten*
C: It'll be about sixty pounds.	

Auf einen BLICK:
Schwerpunkt Simple Present – Die Gegenwart

Simple Present steht, wenn…	Beispiel
etwas oft, regelmäßig geschieht	1. He often *buys* cheap things.
etwas Dauerzustand („Besitz") ist	2. He *has* a wife and four sons.
Verb statisch[2] ist (wie *know, cost*)	3. What does a taxi to H. *cost*?
etwas sich in der Zukunft nach Fahrplan oder Kalender ereignet	4. The next train *departs* at 8:15.
Ereignisse, die aufeinanderfolgen	5. You name it. I *do* it.

1 Anfangsschwierigkeiten 2 Mehr über statische Verben S. 122

H:	Oh, my God. Sixty pounds to *save* thirty or forty euros and fly at a normal time.	*sparen*
B:	Oh, do be quiet, Heidi. Look, we'll rent a car starting this evening *instead of* next week. Come on, *let's get cracking*!	*anstatt* *auf geht's*
	At Heart Car Rentals Pretty young lady behind the counter (**L**)	
B:	We'd like to *hire* a car, please.	*mieten*
L:	It's a bit difficult, Sir. *There's been a rush on* them. From the last *flight* in.	*Ansturm auf* *Flug*
H:	That's typical. What are we going to do? What a start to a holiday!	
L:	I do have one car left. I don't know if it'll *suit* you. It's a Jaguar S.	*passen*
H:	Oh, my God. A *racing car.*	*Rennwagen*
B:	Well, *beggars can't be choosers.*	*keine andere Wahl haben;*
L:	I can give it you with a twenty percent *discount.* That'll be 300 pounds for the week.	*Rabatt*

TEST 1: Kreuzen Sie die falsche Verbform an

1. Your train *is leaving* now.
2. I *know* that this car will suit you.
3. Heidi, *are you having* your driving licence?

TEST 2: Sagen Sie es mit anderen Worten

1. What can I *do for* you?	How can I ____________ you?
2. The next train *leaves* at 8:15.	The next train ____________ at 8:15.
3. What *shall we* do?	What ____ ____ ________ to do?
4. We'd like to *rent* a car.	We'd like to ____________ a car.

Food for thought

It takes over 3,000 bolts and screws[1] to assemble[2] a car – but it takes only one nut to scatter it all over the road.

1 Bolzen und Schrauben, *nut* bedeutet Schraube und Idiot 2 zusammenbauen

B: We'll take it.	
L: Do be careful with it. It's our *top of the range model.* Could I see your *driving licence*?	*Topmodell* *Führerschein*
B: *Here you are.*	*Bitte sehr!*
L: Sir, this is an *odd* licence. No photograph and it's different from the European Union one. I'm afraid I can't accept that.	*sonderbar*
B: Oh, dear me! It's a *temporary* one. Heidi, do you have yours?	*vorläufig*
H: Yes, *fortunately* somebody has the correct documents. Here you are.	*zum Glück*
L: Okay, that's fine. There are a few details I *need*. Where do you live normally? What type of insurance do you *require*?	*brauchen* *benötigen*

TEST 3: Worin unterscheiden sich Satz A und Satz B?

A: Oh, *do be* quiet.	**B:** Oh, *be* quiet.
A: *Do be* careful.	**B:** *Be* careful.

TEST 4: Erinnern Sie sich an das Gegenteil?

1. It's a *permanent* licence.	It's a ____________ licence.
2. They *spent* thirty euros.	They ____________ thirty euros.
3. It's the *same* in Britain.	It's ____________ in Britain.
4. It's *easy*.	It's a bit ____________.
5. It's the *most expensive* one.	It's the ____________ one.

TEST 5: Und welche Verbformen sind hier falsch?

1. Hello, Mr Swindler, I'*m phoning* to book a room.
2. What *are you wanting*? A room for the summer?
3. Sorry, I don't *have* a direct line to heaven.

Our two friends are sitting in the lounge of the airport.

H:	Well, you certainly *let me down* at the car hire, didn't you? How can you *go abroad* when you don't have *valid* documents in your pocket?	*im Stich lassen* *ins Ausland gehen* *gültig*
B:	Heidi, you know how stressful it was. We had to take any plane we could get. My old licence is good enough for Germany.	
H:	Anyway, let's check the *map*. Do you understand these *signs*? What does this symbol *mean*?	*Straßenkarte* *Zeichen; bedeuten;*
B:	I think that is a *nature reserve*.	*Naturschutzgebiet*
H:	My goodness. This looks very complicated. And these are all narrow country roads.	
B:	Don't worry! I'm your *navigator*.	*Lotse*
H:	That doesn't give me *confidence*. Have you at least remembered your *glasses*?	*Zuversicht* *Brille*

Für den Fall, dass Sie ein Auto mieten wollen

Bitte, wo ist hier ein Autoverleih?	Could you tell me where there's a car rental, please?
Wie viel kostet ein VW pro Tag?	How much is the daily rental for a VW?
Sind die Kilometer inbegriffen?	Is the mileage included?
Sie haben keine Kilometerbeschränkung.	You've unlimited mileage.
Ist Vollkaskoversicherung im Preis inbegriffen?	Is fully comprehensive insurance included in the price?
Unsere Autos sind haftpflichtversichert.	Our cars are third-party insured.
Was deckt die Versicherung ab?	What does the insurance cover?
Wie hoch ist die Selbstbeteiligung?	How much is the excess?
Wie hoch ist die Kaution?	How much is the deposit?

Time for a smile

On the motorway at night, a driver is informed by the radio traffic service: "Attention, please. We want to warn you about a driver going in the wrong direction. Please, be careful."
The driver grumbles: "One driver? Hundreds, hundreds ..."

So our two travellers are sitting in a sports coupé. At the moment they are feeling *important*. On the other hand this alternative is *expensive* and they hadn't planned it. The Jaguar is flying *smoothly* along the country roads on the way to Hastings. At this *speed* they will arrive *in less than* an hour.

wichtig · *teuer* · *ruhig* · *Geschwindigkeit* · *in weniger als*

B: Heidi, why are you driving so *fast*? It's really dark along these roads. — *schnell*

H: Well, whose *fault* is it that we're still travelling at this time of the night? And you don't even have a *valid* driving licence here. — *Schuld*, *gültig*

B: I couldn't know that. Now if ... Heidi, *watch out*! There's a *deer* on the road. — *Vorsicht!*, *Reh*

Heidi *hits the brakes* to miss the animal which is crossing the road in front of them. The good news: She *misses* the deer. The bad news: She crashes into a tree at the side of the road. Five minutes later she *comes round.*

auf die Bremse treten · *verfehlen* · *zu sich kommen*

Auf einen BLICK

	Schwerpunkt	Beispiel
1.	Simple or Progressive? Einfache oder Verlaufsform?	She *hits* the deer which *is crossing* the road.
2.	Accidents and formalities	Dial 999
3.	Get to know your car	brake, bonnet and bulb

TEST 1: Bilden Sie Sätze (Vorsicht mit den Verbformen)

1. Tom and Tina / car / in / a / sports / now / sit.
2. Tina / the / along / smoothly / roads /drive.
3. Suddenly / Tina / a / cow / on / see / the / road.
4. Tina / the / brakes / hit.
5. She / the / cow / miss.
6. She / into / a / tree / crash.

Bernd is sitting in the passenger seat *slumped* forward. He is not moving. The car smells of *petrol*. Heidi *felt sick*. She remembers the number 999 for *emergency services*. Twenty minutes later the police arrive together with the *ambulance*.

Ambulance man (**A**), policeman (**P**)

P: Is the *injured* person still *breathing* or is it too late?

A: I'm not sure. I'm just checking now. Let's have a look. Yes, it's probably *concussion*, but there could be *internal bleeding*. His pulse is very weak.

P: You'll want to get him to the *nearest* hospital. From here that'll be Hastings Central. You Miss, I'll have to ask you to *accompany* me to the police station. We can *sort* it all *out* there.

zusammengesackt
Benzin
übel sein
Pannenhilfe
Krankenwagen
Sanitäter
verletzt; atmen
Gehirnerschütterung; innere Blutungen; nächstgelegen
begleiten
klären

TEST 2: Fragewörter

1. ________ are you driving so fast?
2. ________ fault is it?
3. ________ 's the number of the emergency services.

TEST 3: Welche Verbform wählen Sie?

1. They (*drive*) on narrow country roads when suddenly an animal (*jump*) in front of them.
2. Heidi (*look*) after Bernd while the constable (*write*) the report.
3. Bernd (*still breath*) when the ambulance (*arrives*).

TEST 4: Korrigieren Sie die Fehler

P: Do you want a phone?

H: No, I'm still having my mobile.
Oh, good, it rings now.

P: OK. I'm still needing five minutes to write this report.

	Heidi *grabs* their suitcase and goes over to the police car and the *flashing lights.*	*schnappen* *Warnblinkleuchte*
H:	Excuse me, *constable,* I'd like to phone my car rental company.	*Wachtmeister*
P:	Okay. I need five minutes because I'm writing my *preliminary* report. Do you want a phone?	*vorläufig*
H:	No, I have my mobile. Now, what's the number? 01 9543216. Oh, good, it's ringing *at least.*	*wenigstens*
	The clerk (**C**) at Heart answers the phone	
C:	Heart Rentals. Jean speaking. How can I help you?	
H:	I've had an accident. The *bonnet* of the car is smashed up.	*Motorhaube*
C:	Please calm down, Miss. Do you have your rental documents in front of you? What's your number? It's in the *top right hand corner* of the *front page.*	*obere rechte Ecke;* *erste Seite*

TEST 5: Wissen Sie, was das "it" ist?

dashboard • milometer • clutch • petrol gauge • speedometer

It shows how much petrol you have left	____________
It has a glove compartment.	____________
It is a meter that shows your speed.	____________
It is a meter that shows your mileage.	____________
It is a pedal. You press it to change gear.	____________

TEST 6: Was ist das Gegenteil?

a *final report*	a ____________ report
the *bottom left* hand corner	the ____________ hand corner
it takes *more* than an hour	it takes ____________ an hour
a *wide* country road	a ____________ country road

H: Oh, I'm *searching* for it now. Yes, here it is. Number JS.61.	*suchen*
C: Oh dear. It's the Jaguar S. What *bad luck*! Can you tell me *briefly* what happened?	*Pech* *kurz*
H: Yes. We were driving on *narrow* country roads and suddenly there was an animal in front of me.	*eng*
C: Is the car badly damaged?	
H: I think it is. I drove into a tree.	
C: Have you *reported* it to the police?	*melden*
H: Yes, they are writing a protocol now.	
C: Okay. If you look into your *folder* you will find an *accident report* for our insurance. Please fill it out and send it to the address on the *form*. We'll take it from there.	*Mappe* *Unfallbericht* *Formular*

Test 7: Das Auto – Erraten Sie das Kursivgedruckte

1. Could you *fill her up*, please?	______
2. Please change the *bulb* in the *headlight*.	______
3. I've got a *puncture*. Could you fit the *spare*, please?	______
4. Could you *tow* us to the nearest service garage?	______
5. It won't start. Could you *give* it a *push*, please?	______

TEST 8: Für den Fall der Fälle

Welches ist die sinnvolle Reihenfolge? Ergänzen Sie die Lücken

___	Look _____ the injured persons.
___	Fill _____ the accident report.
___	Call 999. Ask _____ an ambulance, if necessary.
___	Wait _____ the ambulance and the police.
___	Report the accident _____ the police.
1	Calm _____.
___	Put _____ warning triangle and a flashing light.

Sticker on an old Mini Cooper:

This was a Rolls-Royce before it went through the car wash.

5 at the police station

Bernd is quickly transported to the Hastings hospital. The police car *follows* with Heidi sitting on the back seat. At the hospital Bernd, who has already *come round*, is made *comfortable*. Doctor (**D**), Heidi (**H**) and the policeman (**P**) in a waiting room.

folgen
zu Bewusstsein kommen; bequem

D: So we've *looked* your *husband over*. There's nothing much wrong. No internal *bleeding*. When did the accident *happen*?

Ehemann; untersuchen; Blutung
passieren

H: I'm not sure. About twelve thirty, I think. Oh, he's not my husband. I'm not *married*.

verheiratet

D: Well, Miss, you might have been killed. *Fortunately*, the Jaguar is a very solid car. By the way, is your boyfriend taking any *medication*?

zum Glück
Medikamente

H: Nothing at all. He never has anything wrong with him. Not even a *headache*.

Kopfweh

D: He'll certainly have a *pain* in his head for the next *couple of days*.

Schmerz
paar Tage

P: Okay, Miss Schmelz, I must ask you to *accompany* me to the station. We could leave now if you're ready.

begleiten

Auf einen BLICK

Schwerpunkte	Beispiel
1. Modale Hilfsverben	We *could* leave now.
2. Past Simple or Progressive?	We *were arguing*.
3. Krankenhaus und Polizei	No *internal bleeding*.

Wichtige *Modal Auxiliaries* (modale Hilfsverben)

er kann / er könnte	he can / he could
er darf / er dürfte	he may / he might
er muss / er musste	he must / he had to
er soll / er sollte	he shall / he should

H: Police station? But I'm not a *criminal.*	*Verbrecher*
P: Well, I'm afraid that can only be *clarified* at the station. After you.	*klären*
Heidi is at the end of her nerves. She *seizes* the suitcase in the waiting room and *strides* towards the door *mumbling* in German. Twenty minutes later they are at the police station. She is sitting *across* the table from Inspector Doubt (**I**) who is questioning her about the accident.	*ergreifen* / *schreiten* / *murmeln* / *gegenüber*
I: Now, Miss Schmelz, I *believe* that's what you said your name was, could you *describe* exactly what happened *in your own words.*	*glauben* / *beschreiben* / *in eigenen Worten*
H: My name is still Schmelz, and *of course* they'll be my words. Nobody can speak for me, can they?	*natürlich*
I: Now then, Miss. Just answer the questions.	
H: I was driving along some country *lane* and *suddenly* an animal ran *in front of* the car.	*enge Landstraße* / *plötzlich; vor*
I: What time was that exactly?	
H: Some time after twelve, I *reckon.*	*annehmen*

Ersatzformen der *Modals* für Vergangenheit, Perfekt und Zukunft

	Ersatzform	Zeiten
can	be able to	he was / has been / will be able to do
may / can	be allowed to	he was / has been / will be allowed to do
must	have (got) to	he had / has had / will have to do

TEST 1: Modale Horrormistakes

	Falsch	Richtig
1. Ich kann Englisch.	*I can English.*	____________
2. Ich kann es.	*I can it.*	____________
3. Du musst es nicht.	*You must not do it.*	____________
4. Er muss es können.	*He must can it.*	____________

Twenty minutes later

I: Forgive me for saying so, but this *whole* thing seems a bit *wishy-washy*. You say you were travelling by car, a luxury car, but you don't know when, you almost *knocked down* an animal, and you don't know what sort it was.

H: I was *tired.*

I: I believe you. That brings me to another point. Why were you driving at that time of night? And in a country you don't know well?

H: Our plane didn't arrive *until* midnight. Then we were *arguing* about what to do so it got very late.

I: Okay. Now what was your boyfriend doing in the car while you were driving? Was he *misbehaving*?

H: He was sitting quite normally.

I: So *neither of you* was drinking any alcohol or anything like that?

H: Of course not.

I: Okay, Miss, we've made a protocol of your *statement.* A police car will take you to your hotel. Give the address to the *constable.*

ganz(e)r
unklar
überfahren
müde
bis
streiten
sich daneben benehmen
keiner von Ihnen
Zeugenaussage
Wachtmeister

TEST 2: *Simple Past* oder *Past Progressive*?

1. We (*drive*) along a road when a deer (*run*) into the car.
2. Neither of us (*drink*) while we (*drive*).
3. We (*argue*) at the time the accident (*happen*).

TEST 3: Lassen Sie sich nicht einschüchtern

Ich weigere mich, auszusagen.	I ______ to ______ evidence.
Hier steht Aussage gegen Aussage.	It's your word ______ ours.
Ich möchte einen Anwalt sprechen.	I'd like to ______ to a ____.
Kann ich eine Kopie des Protokolls haben?	Can I have a ______ of the official ______?

The dynamic young constable (**C**) *takes the chance* to have a conversation with Heidi. She doesn't really feel like talking. She has a headache. They walk round the *back* of the police station to the car.

C: Is this your first time here in England?

H: No, *actually* I visited the U.K. on a student exchange seven or *eight years ago.*

C: Well, I'm sorry you've had such a bad *experience.* But I have to say you *were lucky.* You were driving far too fast on a Sussex country road in the dark. A car could have *collided* with you at any time. There's hardly *space* for two cars to *pass each other.* You can be happy nothing more *serious* happened.

H: I'm not sure. Maybe we were *arguing* at the time. It was a *stupid* situation.

C: Well, shit happens[1] as they say. Oh, here's the car. I'll get you to the hotel in ten minutes. Come on.

die Gelegenheit nutzen
Rückseite
tatsächlich
vor acht Jahren
Erlebnis
Glück haben
zusammenstoßen
Platz; aneinander vorbeifahren; ernst
streiten
dumm

TEST 4: Wohin mit dem Arztvokabular?

breath • insured • prescription • sample
times • vaccinated • waist • X-ray

1. Are you privately ______________?
2. Please get undressed to the ______________.
3. Hold your ______________.
4. Have you been ______________ against tetanus?
5. We need to take an ______________.
6. I need a blood ______________.
7. I'll give you a ______________.
8. Take these pills three ______________ a day.

1 slang

6 no room at the inn

The constable *bundles* Heidi into the police car with a lot of fuss. She just *manages* to grab the suitcase. The car *rushes* along the road with blue *lights flashing and the siren howling*. An *overzealous* constable. They arrive at Holiday Out. There are no lights on at the hotel. Constable Smith presses the doorbell, climbs into his car and *disappears* off into the night. The large wooden door opens and in the *doorframe* appears a figure, tall, thin with a smallish *towel* around his *waist:* Mr Swindler (**S**).

verfrachten
gelingen
dahinrasen; mit Blaulicht und Sirene; übereifrig
verschwinden
Türrahmen
Handtuch
Hüfte

S: What the *devil* is happening? What's all that *noise*? What are the police doing here? Why are you ringing my doorbell at three o'clock in the night? Have you lost your power of *speech*?

Teufel
Lärm
Sprache

Auf einen BLICK

Schwerpunkt	Beispiel
Wortschatzprobleme	*at least* oder *at last*?
Nochmals: Verlaufsform oder einfache Zeit?	I'*m trembling.*
	You need a whisky.
An der Rezeption	Sorry, we're fully booked up.

Time for a smile

Swindler (**S**), guest (**G**)

G: Excuse me, do you have a room for tonight?

S: Certainly, sir. It'll be fifteen pounds a night. Or I can let you have room for only five pounds, if you make your own bed.

G: I'll take the five-pound room.

S: Right, I'll just go and fetch[1] the wood, the hammer and the nails[2] for the bed.

1 holen 2 Nägel

H: *(getting frustrated)* Listen, I *can't get a word in edgeways.* You're asking questions all the time.	nicht zu Wort kommen
S: Well, what do you want here? Do you know what time it is?	
H: *I'm aware* of the time. Could we *at least* go inside. I'm cold.	mir ist klar...; wenigstens
S: She's cold she says. She's at least *wearing something.* I'm the one who's cold. Look at me. I'm standing here with only a *towel* on in the middle of the night. And she says she's cold. My *goose pimples* are so big that they are holding up my towel.	etwas anhaben; Handtuch; Gänsehaut
H: Please.	
S: Alright, alright. Come inside. S.O.S. *Soft* as Swindler!	sanft

Well, at least Heidi is inside the hotel where it is indeed very hot.

TEST 1: Vokabelprobleme aus vorangehenden Kapiteln

near, next oder *nearest?*

Wer ist der Nächste?	Who's ____________?
Wo ist das nächste Hotel?	Where is the ____________ hotel?
Die Bar ist nahe der Rezeption.	The bar is ______ ____ the reception.

ago, before oder *in front of?*

Es geschah vor drei Tagen.	It happened ______ ______ ______
Sie kam vor Mitternacht an.	She arrived ____________ midnight.
Sie wartete vor dem Hotel.	She waited in _______ __ the hotel.

TEST 2: Warum *Simple Present Tense?*

Constable Smith *presses* the doorbell, *climbs* into his car and *disappears.* The door *opens* and a figure *appears* in the *doorframe.*

1. *Simple Present Tense,* weil ________________________________ und
2. *Simple Present Tense,* weil ________________________________

S:	Now, come over here to the *reception desk*, please. Tell me, young lady, what do you *need* from me?	*Empfangsschalter* *benötigen*
H:	Well, we've reserved a room for a week *starting yesterday* evening.	*ab gestern*
S:	Have you? But it's not yesterday evening. It's today in the middle of the night. People often don't arrive after they've *booked*. What's your name?	*buchen*
H:	Schmelz. Heidi Schmelz.	
S:	Schmelz, from August 1st. *Rubbish*! No, I'm sorry, young lady. Not at this hotel.	*Unsinn*
H:	Of course we did! That's *impossible*.	*unmöglich*
S:	No, no Schmelzes here. And we're full anyway. A good hotel gets *lots of* bookings.	*viele*

TEST 3: Noch mehr Wortschatzprobleme?

***lucky, luck* oder *happy, happiness*?**

1. Sie haben Glück gehabt.	You were ________
2. Sie sehen nicht glücklich aus.	You don't look ________ today.
3. Ihre Augen glänzten vor Glück.	Her eyes shone with ________.

***at least* oder *at last*?**

4. Tina must be ________ 70. She is slow but ________ reliable.
5. ________ Tom arrived. I had been waiting for ________ an hour.

TEST 4: Und warum *Simple Present Tense* hier?

People often *don't arrive* after they've booked. You can't *rely* on anybody. They *come* and they *go*. Then nothing *works* any more.

Welche Regel gilt? Wählen Sie!

1. Es handelt sich um Handlungsketten.
2. Swindler benutzt das dramatische Präsens.
3. Er spricht von Situationen, die sich immer wieder ereignen.

H: I'm sure it does. But you sent us a *confirmation.* My goodness, why is it so hot and *humid* here? One minute I'm cold, the next I'm *sweating.*	*Bestätigung* *schwül* *schwitzen*
S: Well, it's your business ...	
H: This is *horrible.* I arrive in England, no *transport,* rent a car, have an accident, my boyfriend Bernd is *injured.* I'm interviewed by the police. The hotel doesn't know me.	*schrecklich; Fahrzeug* *verletzt*
S: You can't *rely on* anybody. Workmen come and workmen go. And then nothing works any more. Whisky?	*sich verlassen auf*
H: Pardon?	
S: You need a whisky, a double whisky. *Here you are*! Bernd, you say. That's a strange name.	*Bitte sehr / Hier bitte*
H: Bernd, Bernd Bubel.	
S: Aha, room six. Why were you talking about Schmelz? Oh, I see. You're not married. Well, breakfast at eight. I wish you a good night.	

TEST 5: Worte an der Rezeption

Für mich ist ein Zimmer reserviert worden.	There is a room ________ for me here.
Wir sind leider ausgebucht.	I'm afraid, we're fully ________.
Wir haben kein Zimmer frei.	We don't have any ________.
Aber Sie haben die Buchung per Fax bestätigt.	But you ________ the booking by fax.
Wie lange bleiben Sie?	How long will you be ________?
Möchten Sie Vollpension oder nur Frühstück?	Do you want________ board or only breakfast?
Gibt es eine Ermäßigung für Geschäftsleute?	Is there a ________ for business-people?
Füllen Sie bitte das Anmeldungsformular aus.	Please fill in the registration ________.
Angenehmen Aufenthalt.	Enjoy your ________.

7 shock after shock

Heidi went up to her room, *suitcase* in one hand, whisky in the other. She *switched* the TV *on* and *lay down* on the bed. There was nothing interesting on any of the four stations. Tired Heidi looked over at the suitcase. "I should *freshen up* and clean my teeth", she said to herself. She got up, put the suitcase on the bed and pressed the *catch*. The suitcase opened. "Wait a minute! This is not ours. Damn, I *picked up* the wrong one when I was waiting at the hospital." Her eyes fell on several notebooks and three *cloth bags*. They were heavy. They seemed to have *balls* or sweets in them. "I know I shouldn't, but what on earth are they?" She *untied* a string and *peeped* in. "Glass stones? No! My God, they're diamonds." Just then somebody *knocked at* the door. "It's five in the morning. Who can that be? It must be that strange Swindler", Heidi thought to herself. "Just a minute!" She opened the door. "Ouch, owwh", she *sighed*, as something sharp and strong-smelling *sprayed* into her face. Her head started to *spin* and she began to fall.

Koffer
einschalten; sich hinlegen
sich frisch machen
Verschluss
abholen
Tuchsack
Murmeln
aufschnüren; blicken
anklopfen
seufzen
sprühen
drehen

Auf einen BLICK

Schwerpunkt	Beispiel
1. Possessivpronomen	They are not *ours.*
2. Wortschatzprobleme	borrow *and* lend
3. Am Telefon	I'd like a number in Hastings.

TEST 1: Die Zeiten begleiten uns weiter

1. She (*picked up*) the wrong suitcase when she (*wait*) at the hospital.
2. She (*switch*) the TV on and (*lie*) down on the bed.
3. Half past ten at the hospital. Bernd (*feel*) good.
4. "I thought you (*want*) to sign out this morning," said the nurse.

Half past ten at the hospital. Bernd was feeling good. He was eating a good English breakfast. That means eggs, *bacon*, tomatoes, *beans* and toast and a strong cup of tea. "I could *get used to* this", thought our hero. Bernd had an *appointment* with Heidi at ten o'clock. At lunch time he was still waiting. "What the hell could have *gone wrong*? She might not have found the hotel. I'll ring Swindler myself." Bernd phones the *operator* (**O**).

halb elf
Speck; Bohnen
sich gewöhnen an
Verabredung
schief gehen
Vermittlung

O: Hello. John Smith speaking. How can I help you?
B: I'd like a number in Hastings.
O: The name of the *subscriber*, please, caller.
B: Well, it's not a person.
O: So it's a *commercial line*?
B: Yes, it's a hotel. It's called "Holiday Out."
O: Okay. The number is 0631 773825. Do you wish to be *connected*?
B: Yes please.
O: Thank you. It's ringing for you now.

Teilnehmer
Firmenanschluss
verbunden werden

After two minutes Bernd gave up. Nobody had *lifted the phone.*

Hörer abnehmen

TEST 2: Kurzformen für Eigentümer

1. The suitcase doesn't belong to *us*.	It's not *ours*.
2. And it isn't *my* suitcase.	It isn't ________.
3. Perhaps it's *Mr Swindler's* suitcase.	Perhaps it's ________.
4. They may be *Mrs Swindler's* jewels.	They might be________.
5. It's not *Bernd and Heidi's* suitcase.	Anyway, it's not ________.
6. And, dear reader, they aren't *your* diamonds either.	They aren't ________ either.

7 shock after shock

Bernd sat on his bed and felt *confused*. Here he was in a *foreign* country. He didn't know where his girlfriend was. He had a *headache* and wanted to go to his hotel. But nobody answered the phone. A young blond-haired *nurse* (**N**) walked into the room.

N: Oh, I'm sorry. I thought you wanted to *sign out* this morning.

B: Well, I did. But my girlfriend hasn't come. And I can't *contact* my hotel. I don't know what to do.

N: Oh dear. I once visited Japan. I know what it is to be alone in a strange place. Is there anything I can do to help?

N: Well, perhaps you could *arrange* a taxi for me. And I don't know *how to put it*, but could you lend me the money for the taxi? I don't have a penny with me.

verwirrt
fremd
Kopfweh
Krankenschwester
entlassen werden
erreichen
kommen lassen
wie ich es sagen soll

TEST 3: Noch mehr Zeitprobleme

1. After Bernd (*leave*) Jenny, he (*think*) about life in general.
2. After two minutes Bernd (*give*) up. Nobody (*lift*) the phone.
3. If you give me your number I (*pay*) you back.
4. If you gave me your number I (*invite*) you to dinner, too.

TEST 4: leihen – *borrow* oder *lend*?

1. A consultant is someone who ______________ your watch to tell you what time it is and then walks away with it.
2. A banker is a fellow who ______________ you his umbrella[1] when the sun is shining and wants it back when it begins to rain.
3. Always ______________ money from a pessimist. He doesn't expect to get it back.

1 Schirm

N: Of course, I can. *No trouble at all.*	*kein Problem*
B: If you give me your number I'll certainly pay you back and I would invite you to dinner, too.	
N: Oh, that's not *necessary.*	*notwendig*
B: Please, it would be a *pleasure.*	*Vergnügen*
After Bernd had left Jenny (that was the nurse's name) he sat down for five minutes and thought about it and his life in general. "Well, that Jenny was so friendly and *relaxed.* No stress. Heidi is always in a *rush.* Always *on the move.* No peace and quiet. Well, that's new for me. Of course, perhaps I *misunderstood* the situation. After all, I'm her patient so she was only doing her job. But *somehow* she made me feel good. Hmm! She's a very attractive woman."	*entspannt* *Eile; auf Achse* *missverstehen* *irgendwie*

TEST 5: Mit der Vermittlung sprechen

Welche Nummer *versuchen* Sie zu erreichen?	What number ________ to get / reach?
Verbinden Sie mich bitte mit Holiday Out.	Please ________ me with Holiday Out.
Ich *verbinde* Sie.	I ________ you through.
Bleiben Sie bitte am Apparat!	________ the line, please.
Tut mir Leid, ich kann ihn nicht *erreichen.*	Sorry, I can't ______ his number.
Die Rufnummer hat sich *geändert.*	The number has been ________.
Die neue Nummer ist ...	The new number is ...
Einen Augenblick. Sie *werden verbunden.*	One moment. It's ________ for you.

Time for a smile

A caller who dials the wrong number will call a second time as soon as you have returned to your living room and made yourself comfortable.

8 Heidi missing

So our charming Bernd managed to get a *date* with Jenny. But first he phones Holiday Out. It's already *late afternoon*. Swindler (**S**), Bernd (**B**).

S: Yes, Holiday Out. Swindler speaking.
B: Hello. My name's Bubel. Bernd Bubel.
S: Well, everyone has his *own cross to bear.*
B: No, I think you misunderstand. I'*m booked* in at your hotel.
S: Right. I'll just ... Right. Yes *indeed.* Well, what about that? What do you have to say for yourself? What was arranged with this hotel?
B: I don't understand. What should I *explain*?
S: Oh, nothing really. Just why you aren't here. Why nobody is here. Why my doors are *left open* in the middle of the night. Why *bills* aren't paid.
B: But my girlfriend was *taken* to your hotel yesterday in the night.
S: Aha! The *famous* Heidi, who's not married, and you're the name on the *registration form*. The boyfriend. Good. Now, what do you have to say *for yourself*? Eh?

Rendezvous
später Nachmittag
sein eigenes Kreuz tragen; eine Reservierung haben
tatsächlich
erklären
offen lassen
Rechnung
bringen
berühmt
Anmeldungsformular
als Rechtfertigung

Auf einen BLICK

Schwerpunkt	Beispiel
1. Passiv	I'*m booked* in at your hotel.
2. Wortschatzprobleme	*bring* or *take*?

Bildung des Passivs

	Subjekt	Verb	Objekt
Aktiv:	Mr Swindler	helps	Bernd.
Passiv:	Bernd	is helped	by Swindler.

Der „Täter" bleibt unerwähnt, wenn unwichtig oder unbekannt.

B: Well, I don't know. I ...
S: Are you coming here to *take this room*, or not? — *das Zimmer nehmen*
B: Of course I am.
S: So, we'll discuss all this when you arrive. Goodbye!

Half an hour later Bernd arrived at Holiday Out. He walked to the reception desk. A *tall* man was standing there, more like a *stick insect* than a human being. — *groß*, *Stabheuschrecke*

S: My name's Swindler. What can I do for you?
B: My name's Bubel.
S: Aha. I've been waiting for you.
B: Well, I *was involved* in a road accident. I was kept in hospital overnight. My girlfriend ... — *verwickelt*
S: The *mysterious* Heidi. — *geheimnisvoll*
B: Yes. She wanted to visit me today. But she never arrived.

TEST 1: Bilden Sie das Passiv

Man nehme eine Zeit von *be* + Partizip Perfekt.

1. An egg is something (*das nie geschlagen wird*[1]) when it is bad.
2. High heels[2] (*wurden erfunden*[3] *von einer Frau*) who didn't like (*geküsst zu werden*) on her forehead[4].
3. A pessimist is a man (*den man gezwungen*[5] *hat*) to live with an optimist.

TEST 2: *eigen = own* – eine Falle für Deutsche

1. Ich sah es mit *eigenen* Augen.	I saw it with ____________ eyes.
2. Ich habe ein *eigenes* Zimmer.	I've got ____________.
3. Sein *eigener* Sohn war der Dieb.	His ____________ son was the thief.
4. Er tat es auf *eigene* Faust.	He did it ____________.

1 beat, beat, beaten 2 hohe Absätze 3 invent 4 Stirn 5 force

8 **Heidi missing**

S:	Well, she certainly arrived here. She was brought here *in splendour.* With lights flashing and sirens *howling.* It was a scandal.	*mit Gepränge* *heulen*
B:	I'm sorry about that, but it's not my *fault.* Okay, I'll go up and see her.	*Schuld*
S:	I very much *doubt* that. She's gone.	*(be-)zweifeln*
B:	What do you mean, "*gone*"?	*verschwunden*
S:	She left in the middle of the night. She *caused* all that trouble, slept in the room and *disappeared* without paying. And she left the room in a *mess.*	*verursachen* *verschwinden* *Saustall*
B:	That can't be possible. This holiday was booked a month ago.	
S:	Are you taking the room now or not?	
B:	Of course I am. The room was reserved by me, myself. Give me the keys!	
S:	"Please" is the word. It *works wonders*!	*Wunder wirken*

Bernd walked *wearily* up the stairs. It was as Swindler had said. The room was *untidy.* There was a strange *smell* and a new brown suitcase. Bernd had no *choice* but to try to be *peaceful* and find out what had happened.

müde
unordentlich
Geruch; Wahl
friedlich / ruhig

TEST 3: bringen – *bring* oder *take*?

1. "Waiter! Waiter! You've (*gebracht*) me a lobster[1] with just one claw[2]!"
"Sorry, sir, it must have lost its claw in a fight."
"Okay, then (*bringen Sie*) this one away and (*bringen Sie*) me the winner."
2. "When I was seven years old my father (*brachte*) me to the zoo."
"Were you accepted[3]?"
3. Soldier: And what happens if the parachute[4] fails to open?
Sergeant: (*Bringen Sie*) it back and you'll get another.
4. But Heidi was (*gebracht*) to your hotel yesterday in the night.
Yes, she was (*gebracht*) here in splendour.

1 Hummer 2 Schere 3 aufnehmen 4 Fallschirm

Bernd didn't know what to do. It was four o'clock in the afternoon. He *decided* to go downstairs and talk to Mr Swindler. — *sich entschließen*

B: You see, Mr Swindler, we had the accident on a Kent country road. And ...

S: ... you were driving like a *racing driver*, I *suppose*. It's your *age*. — *Rennfahrer; annehmen; Alter*

B: No sir, my girlfriend was driving.

S: And suddenly a tree *sprung in front of your car* and hit you? And then you were *knocked* on the head by the tree? — *vor das Auto springen; getroffen werden*

B: And I was taken to hospital by a friendly *ambulance man*. Look, what can I do now? What action should I take? — *Sanitäter*

S: Well, go to the *local* police station. A missing person must be *reported*. Of course, I don't know if they'll *take* you *seriously*. It looks as if you're both trying to *pull all our legs*. — *örtlich; melden; ernst nehmen; sich einen Spaß erlauben mit*

TEST 4: Mr Swindler's passive complaint[1]

Setzen Sie ins Passiv. Verwenden Sie das *Present Perfect*.

1. Bills / *not* / *pay*. — Bills haven't been paid.
2. Doors / *leave* / *open*.
3. The room / *leave* / in a mess.
4. Nothing / *arrange* / with the hotel.
5. The missing person / *not* / *report* / to the police.

Time for a smile

The bearded man stuck a gun in the pilot's back and hissed "I want to be taken to London!"

"But we're going to London anyway."

"I know. But I've been hijacked to Cuba twice before, so this time I'm taking no chances!"

1 Klage

9

9 cuisine at Swindler's

Bernd *spent* the day walking around Hastings. He had *dropped in at* the police-station to report Heidi as a missing person. They seemed to think that our *heroes* must have had an *argument* and that Heidi would simply *turn up* somewhere. In the evening Bernd went back to Holiday Out. His room had not been *cleaned* and he was not really *surprised.* "What am I going to do now?" he wondered. "I *guess* I'll just have to wait at the hotel in the hope that Heidi will suddenly *appear.*"
Bernd was feeling hungry. He had *hardly* had anything to eat in two days with all this stress. "I'll *go downstairs* and order some dinner. We'll see what the restaurant is like." The restaurant was in fact part of the lounge bar and had five or six tables.

verbringen
vorbeischauen
Helden
Streit
auftauchen
sauber machen
überrascht
annehmen
auftauchen
kaum
hinuntergehen

Auf einen BLICK

	Schwerpunkt	Beispiel
1.	Futur mit *will* und *going to*	What *am I going to do* now?
2.	Englisch im Restaurant	I'll take the lamb.

TEST 1: Vergangenheit oder Vorvergangenheit?

1. In the evening Bernd (*go*) back to the hotel. Before, in the afternoon he (*drop*) in at the police-station.
2. His room (*not clean*) and he (*be*) not really surprised.
3. He (*hardly have*) anything to eat in two days with all this stress.

Einfaches *Will-Future* steht für	*Going-to-Future* steht für
A. Voraussagen, Vermutungen **B.** Versprechen **C.** Gewohnheiten, Merkmale **D.** spontane Entschlüsse	**A.** Vorhaben und Absichten **B.** Schlussfolgerungen auf der Basis vorhandener Anzeichen

All the tables were full *except* one where an old lady (**L**) was sitting. Bernd went up to her table. — *außer*

B: Excuse me, madam. Could I *join* you? I'm afraid there are no other tables left. — *Gesellschaft leisten*

L: *Certainly*, young man. You're from room six, aren't you? — *sicherlich*

B: Yes, I am. How did you know that?

L: It's very simple. No great trick, my boy. You see I'm *acquainted* with all the people in the other ten rooms. You're not one of them. So you're from number six. Look, Mr Swindler will be arriving in a few minutes. Have a look at my *menu*. It'll be quicker. — *bekannt*; *Speisekarte*

Bernd looked through the menu. There *certainly* wasn't much *choice*. Two starters, two *main courses* and one *dessert*. — *gewiss*; *Auswahl; Hauptgericht; Nachtisch*

TEST 2: Was bedeutet das einfache *Will-Future*?

Wählen Sie eine Bedeutung aus der Tabelle auf Seite 38: A, B, C oder D?

1. I'*ll take* the lamb.
2. You *will like* it.
3. Swindler is so mean he *will* not *employ* people.
4. At my age *you will* learn to take it easy.

TEST 3: Das *Will-Future* der Verlaufsform, A, B, oder C?

Das *Will-Future* der Verlaufsform steht für eine
A. Situation, die zu einem künftigen Zeitpunkt ablaufen wird.
B. Situation, die sich ereignen wird, weil es selbstverständlich oder so üblich ist.
C. höfliche Frage nach jemandes Plänen.

1. Mr Swindler *will be arriving* in a minute. He always does. ______
2. And, what *will* Sir *be drinking* with it? ______
3. Hello, I know what I'*ll be eating* this evening. ______
4. I'm not sure what I'*ll be getting* now. ______

Swindler (**S**), carrying two *plates* on his arm and almost *dropping* them, is stressed.	*Teller* *fallen lassen*
S: Oh, room number six has *joined* you, Miss Mable (**M**).	*sich jemandem anschließen*
B: Hello, I know what I'll be eating this evening.	
S: Oh, do you, young man. Well, you certainly seem to be in a *hurry.* Couldn't wait for me to bring the *menu*, could you? Young people nowadays, no *patience*!	*Eile* *Karte* *Geduld*
M: Oh, Mr Swindler, I let him have *mine* to *save your legs.*	*meine; Weg ersparen*
S: Hmmph! What will you think of next, Miss Mable? Now Speedy Gonzalez, what can I do for you?	
B: Okay, I'll take the beefsteak with pepper sauce. And ...	
S: Beefsteak?	
B: Yes, beefsteak.	

TEST 4: Der große Zukunftstest für Anti-Muffel

1. Bernd: What *am I going to do* now?
A. spontaner Entschluss oder **B.** Vorhaben?

2. Bernd: *I'll try* the house red.
A. typische Gewohnheit oder **B.** spontaner Entschluss?

3. Swindler: *I won't* be a minute.
A. Versprechen oder **B.** Vermutung?

4. Mable: You're too impatient. You'*re going to get* problems with your blood pressure.
A. Vermutung oder **B.** Schlussfolgerung?

5. Our son *is going to be* an auctioneer[1]. This is the third valuable[2] vase he has brought under the hammer.
A. Schlussfolgerung oder **B.** Voraussage?

6. As soon as the German tourist *gets* to Paradise, he *will ask* for picture postcards.
A. typische Gewohnheit oder **B.** Voraussage?

1 Auktionator 2 wertvoll

S: Oh, you mean beefsteak, as in "beef" and "steak" together. Well, *it's off*!	*es ist ausgegangen*
B: What do you mean "off"?	
S: Off, not on, gone, away, nothing left. The lamb's excellent, *though*.	*allerdings*
B: Okay. I'll take the *lamb*.	*Lamm*
S: Here Mr Bubel, lamb is served with *mint sauce*.	*Minzsauce*
B: Mint. Uhhh! What a mixture!	
S: That is the standard here, Sir. And it will *satisfy* you, too.	*zufriedenstellen*
M: Take a risk, Bernd. It really tastes good.	
S: These young people. They *condemn* before they have even put the *fork* in their mouths. There is a world *beyond* sauerkraut and *sausages*, you know, Mr Bubel. And, what will Sir be drinking with it? Red, white, pink?	*verurteilen*; *Gabel*; *jenseits; Würste*
B: I'll try the house red.	*Hausmarke*
S: Right. *I won't be a minute*. Back again like *a flash of lightning*.	*bin gleich wieder da; wie der Blitz*

TEST 5: Fleisch bei Swindler

1. The meet of an ox is	________
2. The meat of a pig is	________
3. The meat of a baby cow is	________
4. The meat of a deer is	________
5. Mussels or lobster are	________

TEST 6: Ergänzen Sie das Gespräch mit dem Kellner

bill • do • have • put • recommend • starters • take

1. *Haben Sie gewählt?*	*May I ________ your orders?*
2. *Was nehmen Sie als Vorspeise?*	What will you ________ for ________?
3. *Ich kann die Ente empfehlen.*	I can ________ the duck.
4. *Wie ist das Lamm zubereitet?*	How is the lamb ________?
5. *Schreiben Sie alles auf eine Rechnung.*	Could you ________ it all on one ________?

Mr Swindler *runs off.* | *weglaufen*

B: I'm not sure what I'll be getting now.
M: Don't worry, my boy. Swindler is chaotic, but he's okay. He's just so *mean* he won't *employ* people to help him. Let's drink a dry sherry together. Mr Swindler! Two glasses of your dry sherry. | *geizig; einstellen*
S: That's absolutely typical! Why didn't you order it earlier? What am I? A *slave*? Alright, alright. Two sherries for table two. They'll be here in ten seconds if that's fast enough for the *emperor* and *empress* at table two. | *Sklave* | *Kaiser; Kaiserin*

The meal *progressed.* Both of the guests had problems to get what they wanted, but Miss Mable was *on top of the situation.* "At my age you will learn to take it easy. You're too *impatient.* You're going to get problems with your *blood pressure.* You, young sir, seem to be a *case in question.*" Miss Mable had the lamb and Bernd had it, too. That was all there was. But *strangely* enough it *tasted good.* | *seinen Fortgang nehmen; Herr der Lage* | *ungeduldig* | *Blutdruck* | *typischer Fall* | *sonderbarerweise* | *gut schmecken*

Mehr Englisch fürs Restaurant

Könnte ich bitte die Karte haben?	Could I have the menu, please?
Darf ich Ihnen einen Aperitif anbieten?	May I offer you some aperitif?
Was nehmen Sie?	What will you have?
Was würden Sie empfehlen?	What would you recommend?
Ich nehme die Lammkoteletts.	I'll have the lamb chops.
Wie hätten Sie das Steak gern?	How would you like the steak?
Ich schlage vor, wir bleiben beim Rotwein.	I suggest we stay with red wine.
Zum Wohl! / Prost!	Our health! / Cheers!
Wollen wir den Nachtisch jetzt bestellen?	Shall we order the sweet / dessert now?
Hat es Ihnen geschmeckt?	Did you enjoy your meal?

Well, we've already found out a few things about Holiday Out. The warmth, *cosiness*, the varied selection of foods and wines of the best. And our *host*, Mr Swindler? How does he see his services for the *weary* traveller or the naive holiday-maker? To answer this question we did some *research* in a local travel magazine. And this is what we found.

Gemütlichkeit
Gastgeber
müde
Nachforschung

Extract from the *accommodation* adverts in the East Sussex Chronicle:

Auszug; Unterkunft

Wellness another Way!
HOLIDAY OUT

Not one of these typical standardised *boring* hotels where everything works. They're all the same all over the world. Rooms too big, too many *channels* on the TV. Drinks in the *fridge*. Too much luxury! No! Holiday Out does something for your character. It's more of a *survivel course* than a luxury Ritz. You have to do something for your *wellness*. And by doing it you get that wonderful feeling of *achievement*.
Our building is certainly not standard. All rooms have their own design, walls are *bent* (some people say Mr Swindler is *bent*[1], too, but it's only a *rumour*). Windows are *draughty*. At the Old Beggar Bar you can get a glass of Scotch and take it to your room.
Who needs fridges? Evening meal is an *experience*. You'll certainly feel "swindled" after that.
Home entertainment *includes* 4-channel TV. We belong to that group of Englishmen who believe the 4 national channels are better than all the satellitic nonsense that's flying around today.

langweilig
Programme
Eisschrank
Überlebenstraining; Wohlbefinden
Leistung
schräg/krumm
Gerücht
zugig
Erlebnis
umfassen

1 bent = krumm im Sinne von „Krummer Hund"

A menu Swindler's guests can only dream of

Starters – *Vorspeisen*

ham and melon	*Melone mit Schinken*
prawn cocktail	*Krabbencocktail*
smoked salmon	*Räucherlachs*
lobster	*Hummer*

Main course – *Hauptspeise*

Mutton – *Hammel*

lamb	*Lamm*
lamb chops	*Lammkoteletts*
lamb roast	*Lammbraten*

Pork – *Schwein*

cutlet	*Kotelett*
bacon	*Speck*

Beef – *Rind*

beef burgundy	*Burgunderbraten*
brains	*Hirn*
veal	*Kalb*
minced meat	*Hackfleisch*

Poultry – *Geflügel*

roast duck	*gebratene Ente*
roast chicken	*gebratenes Hähnchen*
partridge	*Rebhuhn*
turkey	*Pute*

Game – *Wild*

wild boar	*Wildschwein*
venison	*Reh*
rabbit	*Kaninchen*

Fish	***Fisch***
trout	*Forelle*
perch	*Barsch*
pike	*Hecht*
salmon	*Lachs*
plaice	*Scholle*
sole	*Seezunge*
Vegetables	***Gemüse***
boiled vegetables	*gekochtes Gemüse*
stir-fried vegetables	*Wok-Gemüse*
peas	*Erbsen*
cabbage	*Kohl*
cauliflower	*Blumenkohl*
sprouts	*Rosenkohl*
fried potatoes	*Bratkartoffeln*
chipped potatoes	*Pommes frites*
mashed potatoes	*Kartoffelbrei*
Salad	***Salat***
mixed salad	*gemischter Salat*
cucumber salad	*Gurkensalat*
lettuce	*grüner Salat*
Desserts	***Nachspeisen***
pancake	*Pfannkuchen*
stewed fruit	*Kompott*
fruit salad	*Obstsalat*

Time for a smile

A tourist saw an advertisement for a restaurant which claimed that any dish requested[1] could be served. The man decided to test this restaurant. He entered and ordered an elephant on toast. The waiter took the order[2] and went away into the kitchen. A few minutes later, he returned and said calmly: 'We do apologize[3], Sir, but we have run out of bread[4]'.

1 jedes verlangte Gericht 2 Bestellung aufnehmen 3 um Entschuldigung bitten 4 uns ist das Brot ausgegangen

10 the amateur detective

What a hectic! *Nevertheless* Bernd and Miss Mable get into conversation. All in all Bernd is feeling very depressed. Of course, the *sharp-eyed* Miss Mable has already *noticed* that.

dennoch
scharfäugig
bemerken

M: So you're from Germany? How long have you been here at Holiday Out? I mean you speak very good English.

B: Well, I arrived two days ago. But it's all *gone wrong,* somehow. I've had nothing but *trouble.* I *don't know which way to turn.*

schiefgehen
Ärger; weder ein noch aus wissen

M: You're certainly very *upset.* I think it has something to do with your partner or girlfriend.

durcheinander

B: It certainly does. How did you know that? I haven't *mentioned* it.

erwähnen

M: Of course not. But you have booked into a double when there are enough *singles.*

Einzelzimmer

Auf einen BLICK

	Schwerpunkt	Beispiel
1.	Das Simple Present Perfect	How long have you been here?
2.	Sprachfalle: meinen, glauben	*mean* und *think*
3.	Adverb oder Adjektiv	Describe *exactly* what happened.
4.	Ein Gespräch anfangen	So you're from Germany?

TEST 1: Erkennen Sie ein *Present Perfect*?

	Kurzform: *'s*	Langform: *is* oder *has*?
1.	There's no sign of Heidi.	There _____ no sign of Heidi.
2.	But it's all gone wrong.	But it _____ all gone wrong.
3.	Heidi's disappeared.	Heidi _____ disappeared.
4.	Heidi's a bit impulsive.	Heidi _____ a bit impulsive.
5.	But she's never done anything like that before.	But she _____ never done anything like that before.

B: I see. Well, the *fact* is that we booked a *stay* at Holiday Out and we arrived two or three days ago. I was *involved in* a road accident and spent a day in hospital. When I got out Heidi had *disappeared.*	*Tatsache; Aufenthalt* *beteiligt an* *verschwinden*
M: How very strange! Have you checked the *local* hospitals and the police?	*örtlich*
B: Yes, I've done all that. There's no *sign* of her. I've tried to *imagine* where she could be. She's a bit *fickle*, but she's never done anything like that before.	*Spur* *sich vorstellen* *sprunghaft*
M: Have you had any personal problems with her *recently*? I mean are you two okay together?	*in letzter Zeit*
B: Well, we get on each other's nerves a bit, but nothing special. I'm completely *confused.*	*verwirrt*

TEST 2: *Past Tense* oder *Present Perfect*?

Mable: You (*arrive*) at Holiday Out yesterday.
Bernd: How (*you know*) that? I (*not mention*) it.
Mable: (*you have*) any trouble with Heidi recently?
Bernd: I (*have*) nothing but trouble.
Mable: (*you check*) the local hospital?
Bernd: Yes, I (*go*) there yesterday.
Mable: What (*you do*) since you (*realise*) she had disappeared?
Bernd: Well, I (*not do*) anything sensible so far.

TEST 3: *Mean* oder *think*?

1. Have you had any personal problems with Heidi recently? I ________, are you two okay together?
2. I haven't thrown the suitcase away, but I was ________ about it.
3. How long have you been here at Holiday Out? I ________ you speak very good English.
4. You're upset. I ________ it has something to do with your girlfriend.

During the course of their dinner Miss Mable explains that she is a sort of amateur private detective. She offers her *support* to Bernd who is pretty *desperate.*	*im Verlauf* *Hilfe; verzweifelt*
B: Oh, Miss Mable. You're on holiday here. You don't want to *waste your time* with my problems.	*seine Zeit verschwenden;*
M: My dear Bernd, I may call you Bernd, *mightn't I*? It's my pleasure. It's my hobby.	*nicht wahr / oder?*
B: Well, I can't tell you how *grateful* I am. I'*m at the end of my tether.*	*dankbar; nicht mehr weiter wissen*
M: Now, you describe exactly what happened and what you have done since you realised that Heidi had disappeared. I can imagine that you've had two very *anxious days.*	*bange Tage*
So Bernd did exactly that. He *related* the events one after the other from *his point of view.*	*erzählen* *aus seiner Sicht*

TEST 4: Die richtige Form – Adjektiv oder Adverb?

1. Miss Mable sat *quiet / quietly* for several minutes.
2. Mr Swindler's hotel is not a *quiet / quietly* place.
3. You're *certain / certainly* very upset.
4. I haven't done anything *sensible / sensibly* so far.
5. Nothing worth learning is learned *quick / quickly* except parachuting.

TEST 5: Doppelt genäht hält besser – *mean* oder *think*?

1. Have you ever been to a zoo? I (*meine*) as a visitor?
2. If you (*meinen*) nothing is impossible, try getting your name off a mailing list.
3. He's a guy who can say absolutely nothing and (*meinen*) it.

And when he had finished Miss Mable sat quietly for *several* minutes.	*mehrere*
M: Well, if I have understood the background correctly there are a *couple of things* that we need to do.	*ein paar Dinge*
B: Well, I haven't done anything *sensible* so far. So *I'm all ears.*	*vernünftig*; *ich bin ganz Ohr*
M: Now listen, Bernd. Let's go to the *fireplace* and make our plans. Here's my idea.	*offener Kamin*
Although it was mid-summer and a hot year it was, Mr Swindler had built a *log* fire in the *grate*. There was a real fireside atmosphere. The only problem was that it was twenty-five *degrees centigrade* outside. Bernd began to *sweat*. After five minutes Miss Mable asked him about the *suitcase* in his room.	*Holzscheit; Kaminrost*; *Grad Celsius*; *schwitzen*; *Koffer*
M: You still have it, don't you?	
B: Yes, I haven't thrown it away but I was thinking about it.	
M: Well, could you *pop upstairs* and fetch it?	*hoch laufen*

Ein Gespräch anfangen

Verzeihung, sprechen Sie Englisch?	Excuse me, do you speak English?
Entschuldigung, ist dieser Platz besetzt?	Excuse me, is this seat taken?
Scheußliches Wetter, nicht wahr?	Nasty weather, isn't it?
Es ist ziemlich kalt hier drinnen, finden Sie nicht auch?	It's rather cold in here, don't you think?
Sind Sie zum ersten Mal in Berlin?	Is this your first visit to Berlin?
Darf ich Sie zu einem Drink einladen?	May I invite you for a drink?
Übrigens, ich heiße Meier.	By the way, my name is Meier.
Ich bin aus Bonn. Wo kommen Sie her?	I am from Bonn. Where are you from?
Freut mich, Sie kennen zu lernen.	Pleased to meet you.

11 the talkative suitcase

Bernd *rushed* upstairs and was *fumbling* for his key, when he saw to his *astonishment* that the door stood *ajar*. He had the feeling he wasn't alone. He *pricked up his ears* and listened, but he could only hear the ticking of his alarm clock. He *hesitated*, and then *tiptoed* into the room. Ten minutes later Bernd came running back into the bar.

eilen; fummeln
Erstaunen
angelehnt; die Ohren spitzen
zögern
auf Zehenspitzen gehen

B: I don't understand it. It's *disappeared*. Who would want an *empty* suitcase?
Miss Mable thought for a few seconds.
M: Hmm ... *Who indeed*?
Swindler *pops up* from behind the bar.
S: So, you've come over to the *cosy* fire. Nothing like a good fire. I like to burn *just about everything* there. No need to *waste* money.
M: Mr Swindler, did you *by any chance remove* a suitcase from room number 6?
S: Room number 6? Room number 6!

verschwinden
leer
Wer wohl?
auftauchen
gemütlich
so ziemlich alles
verschwenden
zufällig; entfernen

Auf einen BLICK

Schwerpunkt	Beispiel
1. Past oder Present Perfect?	Problemfall "recently"
2. Sprachfallen	*Listen* oder *hear*?
3. Das Present Participle	He came *running* back.

TEST 1: Verstehen Sie das *Present Participle*?

A. Übersetzen Sie die Kombination *Verb + Present Participle*
B. Nach welcher Verbgruppe steht das *Present Participle*?

1. Bernd *stood listening* at the door.
2. He *came running* back into the bar.
3. He *arrived breathing* heavily.
4. Mrs Mable was still *sitting* at the bar *sipping* her wine.

M: Yes, you remember it. It's the one *located* between number 5 and number 7.	*sich befinden*
S: Oh yes. That number 6. Now I understand. I thought you meant number 6 with a small 6. It's our *broom cupboard*, you know.	*Besenkammer*
M: Mr Swindler! Where's the suitcase?	
S: Well, if you *insist*, it's behind the reception desk. It wasn't being used, so I thought I might sort of, well, sell it. *Waste not, want not*, you know. Money's *short* nowadays.	*darauf bestehen*; *spare in der Zeit, so hast du in der Not*; *knapp*
B: Can I have my suitcase back?	
S: Oh, young sir. So it's *suddenly* yours, is it? Well, alright. Do I have time to serve your drinks or is it a world *disaster*? Okay, okay, I'm going.	*plötzlich*; *Katastrophe*
Now our two detectives have the brown suitcase and two large glasses of red wine in front of them on the bar. Miss Mable brings her *enquiring mind* to *bear on* the problem.	*Neugier; zuwenden*

TEST 2: Erinnern Sie sich? Wie hieß es im Text?

1. Bernd *hurried* upstairs.	Bernd __________ upstairs.
2. He was *searching* for his key.	He was __________ for his key.
3. Did you *take away* the suitcase?	Did you __________ the suitcase?
4. This is a *catastrophe.*	This is a __________.
5. *Save money for a rainy day.*	________ _____ , ________ ____

TEST 3: Sagen – *say, talk* oder *tell*?

1. This suitcase wants to __________ us other things, too.
2. What does our suitcase want to __________?
3. The suitcase __________ very loudly to me.
4. The suitcase is __________ "look at me".
5. It's __________ us that it is a special suitcase.

M: Now, what do we see *in front* of us?	*vor*
B: It's a brown suitcase.	
M: My dear Bernd. Is that all you can see? You've had a university *education* and it seems it hasn't helped you very much.	*Ausbildung*
B: I don't know what you mean. I see a brown suitcase about one metre by seventy-five centimetres.	
M: That's right, of course. But *somehow* this suitcase wants to tell us other things, more *details* about its life and the people around it.	*irgendwie* *Einzelheit*
B: I can't hear anything, I must say, or it's not talking very loudly to me.	
M: That is because you're not listening *attentively.* Now, the suitcase is saying "Look at me. I'm *brand new.* Somebody bought me *recently.*"	*aufmerksam* *nagelneu* *vor kurzem*
Miss Mable opens her bag, takes out a pair of latex *gloves* and a big *magnifying glass.* Bernd looks at her in astonishment. "I don't want to leave my *fingerprints* behind, you know."	*Handschuhe; Lupe* *Fingerabdrücke*

TEST 4: *Past Tense* oder *Present Perfect*?

1. Teacher to pupil: "I (*never lie*) when I was a child."
"So when (*you start*), Sir?"

2. Did you hear about the Scot who (*win*) a holiday for two in Majorca? He (*go*) by himself twice.

3. An intellectual is a man who (*find*) something more interesting than women.

4. "I (*not see*) much of Paul recently. Have you?"
"Yes, I (*meet*) Paul at the club recently."

5. "The suitcase is brand new. Somebody (*buy*) it recently."

➤ ACHTUNG : *recently* ändert die Bedeutung mit der Zeit	
1. mit *Past Tense*	vor kurzem, kürzlich
2. mit *Present Perfect*	in letzter Zeit, seit einiger Zeit

M: It's telling us that it is a special suitcase, a *particular quality*. Look at the leatherwork and the *pocket* inside.	*besondere Qualität; Tasche*
She *inspects* the inside with her magnifying glass. "Aha! Very interesting ... Hmm ..."	*untersuchen*
B: What do you see?	
M: (ignoring Bernd) Now, my brown friend. What is your name? Yes indeed. Leatherwork *Ltd*. And there's an interesting number here, too. 6666.	*GmbH*
B: That's probably only the *production batch* or something like that.	*Serie(nnummer)*
M: We'll see. Now, what else does our *talkative carrier* want to say? I see, a smoker.	*gesprächig; Tragebehälter*
B: Suitcases can't smoke.	
M: No, but their *owners* do. Place your nose into this corner of the case. *Take a deep breath.*	*Besitzer* *tief einatmen*
B: Why, you're right. Tobacco!	
M: Not only the *treacherous weed*. But a very specific one. It's Holland Home. Sweet tobacco. A pipe smoker. *The plot thickens.*	*verräterisches Kraut; der Knoten schürzt sich*

TEST 5: Sprachfalle *hören* – *listen* oder *hear*?

1. Bernd can't __________ anything, because he isn't __________ attentively.
2. He __________, but he could only __________ the ticking of his alarm clock.
3. If you want your wife to __________, then talk to another woman.
4. There are only two kinds of bosses who fail: those who __________ to nobody and those who __________ to everybody.

12 the chase begins

Miss Mable and Bernd *made an appointment* to meet each other the following day. The dynamic duo *needed* to find out where the leather company *was located.*	*sich verabreden* *müssen* *sich befinden*
M: Listen, let's go to the *Registry of Company Names for England*. It's in London. Now you could find out when the next ...	*Handelsregister*
B: (*interrupting*) Miss Mable. It's not necessary. We can get the information through the Internet. Let's find Swindler. He can *provide* us with computer *access.*	*unterbrechen* *Zugang verschaffen*
M: My goodness, you young people have been working with the new media for years and I'm just a dinosaur. I can't *manage with* computers and videos and all that electricity. I've been living on this planet for almost seventy years and I won't change my *ways* now.	*umgehen mit* *Gewohnheiten*
B: You don't need to. I'll *deal with* all that.	*sich kümmern um*

Auf einen BLICK

Schwerpunkt	Beispiel
1. Present Perfect Progressive	He'*s been working* all day.
2. Sprachfallen: Was ist richtig?	Sorry. What *have* you *said*? Sorry. What *did* you *say*?

TEST 1: Termine – *appointment, date* oder *deadline*?

Richtig (**R**) oder Falsch (**F**)?

	R	F
1. I've got an *appointment* with my girlfriend tonight.		
2. I'd like to make an *appointment* with your doctor.		
3. Call my secretary and arrange a *date.*		
4. The *appointment* for applications is 30 April.		
5. Should we set a *date* for the next meeting?		

They walk over to the reception desk where Swindler is *fumbling* with a telephone. — *herumfummeln*

S: Damn technology! It never *works* when you need it. Might as well send a *pigeon*. It's quicker. Yes, room six, what do you want from me now? — *funktionieren*, *Taube*

B: Sorry to *bother* you, Mr Swindler, but we need a computer with *access to the Internet.* — *belästigen*, *Internetzugang*

S: Well, that's a computer! Not a simple computer. Oh no! The *gadget* has to have access to the Internet. Have you any *notion* what a computer costs? — *Spielerei*, *Vorstellung*

B: Normally it's *all part* of the service. I ... — *dazugehören*

S: (interrupting) Service? The problem with service is that *every Tom, Dick and Harry* thinks he has the right to get everything. I've been serving you drinks all week. That's service! I serve you dinner. But you want more. You want Internet and God knows what. — *Hinz und Kunz*

B: I *take* it that you're not on-line then? — *daraus schließen*

TEST 2: *Present Perfect Simple* oder *Progressive*?

- *Present Perfect Simple* steht oft für Situationen, die noch andauern bzw. deren Ergebnisse.
- *Present Perfect Progressive* betont, dass Aktivitäten ununterbrochen / immer noch andauern – oft bei Zeitangaben mit *since* oder *for*.

Streichen Sie die unpassende Form.

1. No woman *has ever shot / has ever been shooting* her husband while he was doing the dishes.

2. My wife *has been missed / has been missing* for two days. I don't know whether she has left me or gone shopping.

3. An intellectual is a man who *has found / has been finding* something more interesting than women.

4. Tina *has taken / has been taking* these anti-fat pills for months. Now she's so thin that every time she walks in the park, a dog tries to bury her.

Bernd and Miss Mable have been walking around for more than an hour looking for an Internet café. Bernd is *discouraged*. Then he has a *brainwave*. "I'll phone Jenny. Perhaps she can help." — *entmutigt; guter Einfall*

One hour later they are sitting in Jenny's living room in her small apartment which is *located* in Battle, a small town near Hastings where the Battle of Hastings *actually took place*. "And some of the people look as if they had been in that *battle* one thousand years ago," thought Bernd. — *sich befinden*; *tatsächlich; stattfinden; Schlacht*

J: You've been sitting in front of that computer more than half an hour. Have you found the information you want?

B: Yes, indeed I have. *Hold on* a minute. I'll just print it out. There we are. — *Warte!*

M: What does it say? Where is Leatherworks?

TEST 3: *Present Perfect Simple* oder *Progressive*?

1. Mr Swindler (*besitzt*) the hotel (*seit zwei Jahren*).
2. Mr Swindler (*hat serviert*) drinks (*die ganze Woche*).
3. Mr Swindler (*hat schon gehabt*) many guests from Germany.
4. Young people (*arbeiten*) with the new media (*seit Jahren*).
5. They (*sitzen*) at the computer (*seit einer Stunde*).
6. The company (*ist tätig*) in Bournemouth (*seit 1995*).

TEST 4: Wortschatz Power. Wie wurde es gesagt?

1. I won't change my *life* now.	I won't change my _____ now.
2. I can't *handle* computers.	I can't _______ *with* computers.
3. Have you any *idea* what computers cost?	Have you any _______ what computers cost?
4. Then Bernd has a *brilliant idea*.	Then Bernd has a ___________.

B:	*According to this* the company *has been operating* in Bournemouth since 1995.	*demnach; tätig sein*
M:	That's just an hour from here by train. Let's go to the railway station. It's only *a stone's throw away*.	*Katzensprung*
J:	Yes, and it's a lovely day so the *walk* will do you good.	*Spaziergang*
M:	Yes, we've certainly been having beautiful *weather* round here.	*Wetter*
J:	Well, it's mostly clear. In the winter not too cold and windy. In summer blue skies. We have more days of sun than most other *parts* of England.	*Gegend*
M:	I suppose it's the *influence* of the Gulf Stream.	*Einfluss*
B:	Okay, *we ought to be off*. Jenny, don't forget we have an *appointment* on Friday evening.	*wir sollten aufbrechen; Termin*
J:	You mean a *date*. I'm not your doctor.	*Verabredung*
M:	Hmmm! I see you're getting into the local culture. Very *enterprising*.	*unternehmungslustig*

TEST 5: Zeiten – Sprachfallen für Deutsche

	Deutsch	Falsch	Richtig
1.	Ich habe ihn im Bus gesehen.	I *have seen* him on the bus.	I ___________ him on the bus.
2.	Ich habe ein Jahr in Bonn gewohnt.	I *have lived* in Bonn *for a year.*	I ________ in Bonn *for a year.*
3.	Ich wohne seit einem Jahr in Bonn.	I *live* in Bonn since a year.	I _________ in Bonn *for* a year.
4.	Wartest du schon lange?	*Are you waiting* (*for*) long?	____________ (for) long?
5.	Was hast du gesagt?	*What have you said?*	*What* __________?

13 detectives on the move

At Battle Railway station Mable and Bernd *queue up* at the *ticket counter.* It's difficult for Bernd to stand *peacefully* in line and wait. He feels impatient. *Eventually* it's his turn. Ticket clerk (T).

sich anstellen
Fahrkartenschalter
ruhig/friedlich
schließlich

B: Two tickets to Bournemouth, please.
T: Two tickets? Single or *return*?
B: Return, please.
T: Will you be staying there more than two days? If yes, you can get a *discount* of twenty percent.
B: No, we'll only be *a couple* of hours in Bournemouth. Could you give us *a few departure times*?
T: Yes, of course. Trains depart *on the hour* for Bournemouth from platform 9. First or second class?
M: We'll take second class. Thank you.

hin und zurück
Rabatt
ein paar
ein paar; Abfahrtszeiten; jede volle Stunde

On the train, which was very dirty *by anyone's standards*, the *ticket collector* (**T**) soon found the strange *couple.*

auch für bescheidenste Ansprüche
Schaffner; Paar

Auf einen BLICK

Schwerpunkt	Beispiel
1. Das Passiv	Our suitcases *are damaged.*
2. Mit dem Zug reisen	A single to London.

TEST 1: Kaufen Sie eine Fahrkarte

Eine Fahrkarte nach London, bitte.	A ________ to London, please.
Einfach oder hin und zurück?	Single or ________?
Zweimal einfach nach Cardiff, bitte.	Two ________ to Cardiff, please.
Erster oder zweiter Klasse?	________ or ________ class?

T: Tickets please.

B: *Here you are.*

T: Hmmm. How long have you been sitting in this *compartment*?

M: About half an hour, I *suppose*. Why do you want to know?

T: Well, you've been using first class *facilities* with a second class ticket. There will be a *surcharge* of seven pounds per person.

B: But the *carriage* is shabby. It can't be first class. What on earth does the second class look like?

T: Young man, you seem to see everything when it comes to *dirt*, but you can't read the big number one on the window next to your *seat*. Come along, you two. *Pay up*!

Hours later. Miss Mable had a red *face*. "How *embarrassing*. That has never happened to me before." Bernd wasn't too *worried* about it. "Let's get a taxi to the leather shop. It's costing us too much time." Ten minutes later they were standing in front of a large shop with a *board* in the shop window. The words were *written* in gold on *leather*.

Bitte sehr
Abteil
annehmen
Einrichtungen
Zuschlag
Wagon
Dreck
Sitzplatz
Bezahlen Sie!
Gesicht; peinlich
besorgt
Tafel
schreiben; Leder

TEST 2: Englisch für den Bahnhof

break • change • connection • delayed • platform • through

Der Zug aus X hat eine Verspätung von 15 Minuten.	The train from X is ________ by 15 minutes.
Erreiche ich meinen Anschlusszug in X noch?	Will I be able to catch my ________ in X?
Kann ich die Fahrt unterbrechen?	Can I ________ the journey?
Muss ich umsteigen?	Do I have to ________?
Nein, es ist ein durchgehender Zug.	No, it's a _ ________ train.
Von welchem Bahnsteig fährt mein Zug ab?	Which ________ does my train leave from?

LEATHERWORKS LTD. IN BOURNEMOUTH	
ANYTHING in leather.	
Our prime quality *hides* are	*Häute*
stained* and *dyed	*beizen; färben*
to your *wishes*.	*nach Wunsch*
Every *piece* is hand-made.	*Stück*
Our *range* includes:	*Kollektion*
★ handbags, *purses, briefcases,* suitcases	*Geldbörsen; Akten-*
of every style and *size*	*koffer; Größe*
★ leather jackets of high quality	
★ travelling bags	
★ many different *accessories*	*Zubehör*
All our products are *customised*	*maßgefertigt*
and individually numbered.	

TEST 3: Fragen Sie nach der Abfahrtszeit

Wann fährt der Zug ab?	When does the train ________?
Könnten Sie mir ein paar Abfahrtszeiten nennen?	Could you tell me a ______ ______ times?
Kommt der Zug pünktlich an?	Will the train be ____ ____?
Die Züge fahren jede volle Stunde.	Trains depart ___ __ ____.

TEST 4: *Will-Future Simple* oder *Progressive*?

Will-Future Progressive
besteht aus *will*+*be*+Verb in der *ing*-Form;
man nimmt es oft für höfliche Fragen.

1. (you *stay*) there more than two days?
2. No, we (only *be*) a couple of hours in Bournemouth.
3. (you *travel*) first or second class, sir?
4. We (*take*) second class.
5. (you *pay*) cash or by credit card, sir?
6. (you *come*) back on the same train, sir?

Our two amateur detectives *stare at* the board.	*starren auf*
M: Well, *it would seem* that we've come to the right place. Our suitcase is certainly a quality product.	*es scheint so*
B: Well, let's go in and see if we can get some information.	
They enter the shop through a heavy wooden door that Bernd *struggles* to push open.	*sich abmühen*
B: Jesus, you need to be a professional *weightlifter* to get into here.	*Gewichtheber*
M: Didn't you tell me you do a lot of sport back in Germany?	
B: Yes, but it's table tennis and *skittles.*	*Kegeln*
The whole place smells of leather and *various* polishes. There is a *huge assortment* of leather goods – some very strange *shapes* indeed. An old fellow *shuffles* into the shop from a *backroom*.	*verschiedene* *riesiges Sortiment* *Formen; schlurfen* *Hinterzimmer*

TEST 5: Setzen Sie ins Passiv

Form: eine Zeit von *be* + Partizip Perfekt
Gebrauch: das Ergebnis ist wichtig oder der „Täter" anonym

1. They stain and dye the leather. The leather __________ and _____
2. They customise all products. All products ______________.
3. They number the suitcases. The suitcases ______________.
4. They make every piece by hand. Every piece ______________.

TEST 6: Passiv zum Schmunzeln

1. A man who steals a horse (*put*) into prison; a man who steals a whole country (*made*) king.
2. A pessimist is a man who (*force*) to live with an optimist.
3. High heels (*invent*) by a woman who didn't like to be kissed on her forehead.

14 following the trail

So there they are: Miss Mable, Bernd and a *shabbily* dressed gentleman. They *look each other over* for twenty or thirty seconds before anybody says anything. The old *craftsman* (**C**) is clearly the *proprietor* of the shop.

C: Hello, you two. How do you do, young sir, and madam, the mother, I *presume*?

M: Your *presumptions*, my good man, could not be more wrong. I have no son, and have never been married, and *moreover* I have not *regretted* this status.

C: Oh, I *apologise* most sincerely. A silly *prejudice* on my part.

M: Your *apology* is accepted. Now ...

B: (interrupting) Do you know this suitcase?

C: Know it, young man? I *spent* a month working on it. There's no *defect* in the *workmanship*, I *trust*?

schäbig
sich mustern
Handwerksmeister; Eigentümer
vermuten
Vermutung
darüber hinaus
bereuen
sich entschuldigen; Vorurteil
Entschuldigung
verbringen
Fehler; Handwerk
hoffen

Auf einen BLICK

	Schwerpunkt	Beispiel
1.	Adjektiv oder Adverb?	*clear* oder *clearly*
2.	Übersetzung von *müssen*	*must, need,* oder *have to*
3.	Sprachfallen	*remind* oder *remember*

TEST 1: Wählen Sie aus! Adjektiv oder Adverb?

correct • correctly • shabby • shabbily • clear • clearly

1. The gentleman was __________ the owner of the shop.
2. Miss Mable tried to keep a __________ mind.
3. And he looked __________.
4. He was __________ dressed.
5. The gentleman didn't understand __________.
6. His behaviour was __________.

M:	We need to know who bought this *priceless* piece from you. His name must be *recorded* somewhere. Certainly an *invoice* will be *filed* somewhere here in your shop.	*kostbar* *festhalten* *Rechnung; zu den Akten legen*
C:	Invoice? Well, I can't give out that sort of information.	
B:	Listen, my girlfriend may well be locked up somewhere, if not *worse*. She's *disappeared*.	*schlimmer; verschwunden; ungeduldig*
M:	My *impatient* young friend is trying to explain that we very much need to know who bought this suitcase. The *owner* should be identified and *screened*. He may be a *criminal*.	*Eigentümer; überprüfen; Verbrecher*
C:	Okay. I understand. A customer number must have been *printed* into the piece somewhere. Let me see. Ah, here it is. 6666. Let me check my *customer records*. Yes! 6666. Inspector John Reed. 14 Castle Road, Dover.	*drucken* *Kundenkartei*
M:	Inspector, as in police inspector? Have I understood correctly? Is Mr Reed a member of the *constabulary*?	*Polizei (-truppe)*

TEST 2: Wortschatztraining

The verb	And the noun?	
know	______________	Wissen
presume	______________	Annahme
apologize	______________	Entschuldigung

TEST 3: Worte der Entschuldigung

Die Wörter sind durcheinander geraten. Korrigieren Sie die Fehler.

1. *Apologize* me, what time is it, please?
2. I *excuse* for that stupid remark.
3. I'm sure you have some lame *apologies* for not coming.
4. Please accept my sincere *excuses*.

14 following the trail

C: Yes, ma'am and a pipe-smoker. I remember him well. He had one of those Dutch *clay pipes*. And sweet tobacco like we *used to* get on the black market, from Holland. And a real gentleman he is. Tweed jacket and he was wearing a tweed cap, too. I didn't like his friend, *though.*

M: Friend? What was the problem with him?

C: Well, he spoke *dreadful* English. And he looked shabby. He smelled of fish.

M: Dreadful English? A *foreigner*?

C: No, he was an East Ender. A Londoner.

M: Hmmm! A *gentlemanly* policeman and a fellow from the slums of London.

The two amateur detectives *left* the shop somehow depressed. Well, it's not every day that you find out that the *guardians of law and order* might not be as perfect as you had thought.

clay pipes – *Tonpfeife*
used to – *pflegen*
though – *jedoch*
dreadful – *fürchterlich*
foreigner – *Ausländer*
gentlemanly – *vornehm*
left – *verlassen*
guardians of law and order – *Hüter von Recht und Ordnung*

TEST 4: Müssen – *must, need* oder *have to*?

1. The inspector's name ___________ be recorded somewhere.
2. Our detectives *will* ___________ visit the man in Dover.
3. We ___________ to know who bought the suitcase.

Und nun etwas zum Schmunzeln:

4. "Do you serve women in this bar?"
   "No, sir, you (*müssen*) bring your own."
5. I (*nicht müssen*) tell my wife anything.
   My neighbours do it for me.
6. There are two kinds of men: those we may dream about and those we (*müssen*) marry.

TEST 5: Erinnern – *remember* oder *remind*?

1. The old craftsman _________ the inspector well.
2. Something _________ Bernd of Jenny.
3. I can't _________ your name, and please don't _________ me!

Miss Mable had mixed feelings on the *subject.* "Okay, we'll have to visit the man in Dover and see if we can *puzzle out* what is going on. A person is innocent until *proven guilty*, at least in this country."

Sache / Thema
austüfteln
für schuldig finden

Bernd was *surprised* that they could get the information so easily. Well, *at least* they had a possible next *step*. Perhaps it would *lead* to them finding Heidi. "Ah yes, Heidi. Hmmm. Well, that *reminded* him of Jenny. Okay, one thing after another. I'd better give Jenny a phone call. *After all* they had arranged a dinner date together. Oh, my goodness, I've nothing at all to *wear*." These were the things which *were on* Bernd's *mind.*

überrascht
wenigstens
Schritt; führen
erinnern
schließlich
anziehen; beschäftigen

Miss Mable still could not get it clear in her head. A policeman *involved* in all this business? "There could be many *reasons* for that", she thought. "Perhaps it's something *undercover.* Maybe it's a totally innocent situation. And, of course, what if a '*copper*' had gone bad? It wouldn't be the first time." Well, *in any case* now they had his address.

beteiligt
Gründe
verdeckte Ermittlung; Bulle
jedenfalls

TEST 6: Erinnern Sie sich an die Gegenteile?

1. Miss Mable didn't *reject* the apology. She ___________ it.
2. Maybe Mr Reed is *innocent*, maybe he is ___________.
3. Bernd should be more *patient*. He is too ___________.

TEST 7: Typisch deutsche Fehler. Korrigieren Sie!

1. There's no mistake in the workmanship, I hope.
2. Is Mr Reed member of the constabulary?
3. A person is innocent until proven guilty, at last in England.
4. Miss Mable is having no son, and has never been married.
5. Bernd was surprised that they could get the information so easy.

15 plenty more fish in the sea[1]

Miss Mable and Bernd take the train back to Hastings and Holiday Out to plan which steps to take next. As we know Bernd is thinking about other things. He takes out the piece of paper with Jenny's telephone number on it. It's the number at the hospital. *Operator* (**O**). — *Vermittlung*

B: Hello, is that the hospital? I'm sorry, I'm trying to contact Jenny Walsh.

O: Miss Walsh? Do you know which *ward* she is on? — *Station*

B: Well, she's a *nurse.* I think she's in the accident ward. At least she *took care of* me when I had my accident. — *Krankenschwester*, *sich kümmern um*

O: Okay, I'm *putting you through* now. It's ringing for you, *caller.* — *verbinden*, *Anrufer*

Bernd soon *got through* to Jenny (J) who seemed happy to hear his *voice.* — *verbunden werden*, *Stimme*

Auf einen BLICK

Schwerpunkt	Beispiel
1. Das Question Tag	You found your shop, *didn't you*?
2. Englisch gegen Geldnot	I've run out of cash.

Das Question Tag

- Das *Question Tag* nach einer Aussage entspricht dem deutschen *oder, nicht wahr*. Es steht in der Zeit des Verbs, das es vertritt.
- Hilfsverben werden im *Tag* wiederholt. Vollverben im *Simple Present* und *Simple Past* werden durch *do, does, did* ersetzt.
- Ist das Verb bejaht, so ist das *Tag* verneint. Ist das Verb verneint, so ist das *Tag* bejaht.

1 Andere Mütter haben auch hübsche Töchter

J: Hi, Bernd! Nice to hear from you so soon. You found your shop, didn't you?

B: Yes, we certainly did. It was an *old-fashioned leather-wear* shop. Just like in the old days. — *altmodisch; Lederwaren*

J: I *suppose* they didn't want to give you any private information, did they? — *vermuten*

B: Well, at first it was a bit *tricky*, but then when I explained how *serious* the *matter* was the old *proprietor* gave us everything we needed. — *schwierig; ernst; Sache; Besitzer*

J: You don't mean you know where your *fiancée* is, do you? — *Verlobte*

B: Eh, listen, Heidi and me, we're not *engaged*. She's just, well, my girlfriend. Well, it's nothing serious. I mean, well, you know what I mean, don't you? — *verlobt*

J: Hmmm. I think I'm beginning to *get the picture*. Anyway, when are we meeting? — *klar sehen*

B: Oh, right. Tomorrow evening. Listen, there's a very good restaurant in Battle near Hastings. It was *recommended* by Miss Mable, and she's a lady who knows what's she's talking about. About eight o'clock will be okay, won't it? — *empfehlen*

TEST 1: Korrigieren Sie die Fehler in den *Tags*

1. You *found* your shop, *did you*?
2. They *didn't want* to give you any information, *didn't they*?
3. See you tonight. Eight o'clock *will be* okay, *isn't it*?
4. Bernd *had done* everything he could to find Heidi, *didn't he*?

Ergänzen Sie die *Tags* zum Schmunzeln

5. "Waiter, there's a dead fly in my soup."
   "Well, for 50 pence you don't expect a dead eagle[1], __________?
6. The oldest joke we know is when Eve asked Adam, "You love me, __________?" and he replied, "Who else[2]?"

1 Adler 2 Wen sonst?

Well, dear reader, perhaps you have *noticed* that Bernd, the *red-blooded* young fellow, has *got the hots* for Jenny. (By the way, this condition is not only *limited* to young fellows.) Indeed Bernd is shocked how fast things have moved. "My goodness, so much has happened and I've only been here for a few days. *Somehow* I have some *strange* feelings inside me. I feel different from a week ago."

Bernd was not thinking about Heidi. "Well, she'll *manage okay*. She always does." To tell the truth Jenny was on his mind. He was *excited* about meeting her. Strange because he *tended to* plan things for the future and she certainly hadn't been in his plans. In a way he began to feel *guilty*. "I should be doing more to find Heidi." But he had done everything he could, hadn't he?

"Okay", thought Bernd. "I can't change the situation. Let's live for the moment." Then with sudden *realisation* he noticed what he was wearing. The same old jeans and sweater that he had *started off* with in Germany. "Oh, my God. How *grubby*! How shabby."

bemerken
vollblütig; verknallt sein in; beschränkt
irgendwie; eigenartig
zurechtkommen
aufgeregt
neigen zu
schuldig
Erkenntnis
aufbrechen
schmutzig

TEST 2: Englisch gegen Geldnot. Ergänzen Sie

cash • change • draw • rate • run

Ich habe kein Bargeld mehr.	I have ________ out of cash.
Ich hätte gerne für 500 Euro Britische Pfund	I'd like to ________ 500 euros into pounds.
Wie ist der Wechselkurs heute?	What's the ________ today?
Wo ist bitte der Geldautomat?	Where is the ________ dispenser?
Kann ich Bargeld mit meiner Kreditkarte abheben?	Can I ________ cash with my credit card?

All these things were *passing through* Bernd's *mind* as he was sitting in a pub in Hastings. "I *need* money. I *need to* get some fresh clothes. I only have an EC card. Heidi always told me that wouldn't work *abroad.* She has the other cards. I'll try it *anyway.*" Bernd went to a *cash dispenser* at Barclays. He looked into the small screen. "Please *choose* your language": Bernd pressed English.	*durch den Kopf gehen; brauchen* *müssen* *im Ausland* *einfach* *Geldautomat* *wählen*
"Would you like cash or a *statement of your account?*" Bernd pressed "cash".	*Kontostand*
"Please *enter* your pin number and then *confirm* by pressing the green *key.*" Bernd did it. Next the machine asked him how many pounds he wanted to *withdraw.* He *cheekily* entered a thousand pounds. After a while the message *flashed up*:	*eingeben; bestätigen; Taste* *abheben* *frech* *aufleuchten*
"Your *request* is being *processed.*"	*Auftrag; bearbeiten*
One minute later Bernd had a thousand pounds in his *sweaty* hands. "My God, it really worked. Now I can really *smarten* myself *up.*"	*verschwitzt* *sich fesch machen*

TEST 3: Probleme am Geldautomaten

Setzen Sie die Verben in die richtige Form.

Der Automat hat meine Karte einbehalten.	The machine (*take*) my card.
Haben Sie die richtige Geheimnummer eingegeben?	(you *type*) in the correct pin?
Ich fürchte, Sie haben Ihr Konto überzogen.	I'm afraid you (*overdraw*) your account.
Ich habe meine Kreditkarte verloren. Was soll ich tun?	I (*lose*) my credit card. What shall I do?
Sollen wir Ihr Konto sperren?	(we *bar*) your account?

16

16 dinner for tw

Feeling almost like a new man Bernd walked down towards the old town. On the way he quickly *dropped into* Mucks&Spunsers and *drifted into* the menswear department. He didn't want to spend too much, but he had to look normal for his date with Jenny *at least.* Well, life goes on. Shop assistant (**S**).	*reinschauen* *schlendern* *Rendezvous; wenigstens*
S: How can I help you, sir?	
B: Well, I'm looking for a pair of *trousers*, a shirt and a pullover.	*Hosen*
S: Of course, sir. What *size* trousers do you take?	*Größe*
B: I *take a fifty*, I think. I'm not sure what that is here in England.	*Größe 50 haben*
S: Let's see, I'll just check it here in the list. That's a forty here in the *U.K.* What type of trousers would you like?	*United Kingdom*
B: I was thinking of cord trousers in brown, *slim cord. Slim*-line style.	*Feinkord* *schlank*
S: Yes, we have them. Here you are. You can try them on in the *cubicle.*	*Umkleidekabine*
(Five minutes later, Bernd comes out happily)	

Auf einen BLICK

Schwerpunkt	Beispiel
Adjektiv oder Adverb?	*happy* oder *happily*
Sprachfallen	eventuell bedeutet nicht *eventual*
English for dinner and shopping	Are you ready to order, sir?

TEST 1: Übersetzen Sie. Adjektiv oder Adverb?

1. Bernd (*schnell*) drops into Mucks&Spunsers.
2. He wants to look (*normal*).
3. Five minutes later Bernd comes out (*glücklich*).
4. He is (*glücklich*) to have found the right outfit for the date.
5. The new clothes fit (*perfekt*).

B: Okay. They *fit* perfectly. And I'll need a shirt and pullover *to match.* I've got a date.	*passen* / *passend dazu*
S: Well, I'm sure she'll *fancy* you in this stuff. Good luck!	*mögen*
She gave him little *table* to help him and some information about shopping. He slept well that night and *eagerly* looked forward to his date. Anyway, Bernd didn't have any problems with money.	*Tabelle* / *begierig*
Saturday evening came very slowly. But come it did *eventually*. Our hero had got himself *spruced up* for his date.	*schließlich; sich schön machen*
Bernd entered the restaurant rather nervously. He looked around *casually.* There was an empty table in one corner a few yards away from an *open fire* which was *crackling* away. A young waitress (**W**) dressed elegantly in black *approached* him.	*lässig* / *offener Kamin* / *prasseln* / *sich nähern*
W: Have you reserved a table, sir?	
B: Yes, I have. *In the name of* Bubel.	*auf den Namen*
W: Bubble? Hmmm. How do you *spell* that please?	*buchstabieren*
B: Yes, it's Bee yu double bee el, Bubel.	

TEST 2: English for the clothes shop

Setzen Sie die Wörter ein. Manche müssen verändert werden.

alter • fit • nice • serve • size • take • wonder

Werden Sie schon bedient?	Are you being ________?
Könnten Sie mir vielleicht helfen?	I ________ if you could help me.
Was für eine Größe brauchen Sie?	What size do you ________?
Ich fürchte, dieser Anzug sitzt nicht gut.	I'm afraid this suit doesn't ________ me very well.
Man kann es ändern, ohne Aufpreis.	It can be ________ at no extra charge.
Diese Bluse passt gut zu Ihrem Rock.	This blouse goes ________ with your skirt.
Ich brauche die nächste Größe.	I need the next ________ .

W: Yes sir. Here's your table near the fire. Will your company *be long*? Perhaps you would like an aperitif?	*spät kommen*
B: Yes please. I'll take a dry sherry. Ah, here's my friend now.	
Bernd and Jenny drink their aperitifs slowly enjoying some small talk.	
J: The fire's wonderful, isn't it? So *cosy.*	*gemütlich*
B: It *certainly* is.	*sicher*
W: Would you like to *order* now. I *believe* you have the *menu.*	*bestellen; glauben* *Speisekarte*
The evening menu at Pilgrims was relatively simple. To *cut a long story short* Jenny chose some *smoked salmon paté* with hot toast. Bernd preferred *deep-fried breaded Brie.*	*kurz gesagt; Lachspastete; frittierter Käse*
B: What do you fancy for your *main course*? I think the *breast of duck* sounds very good.	*Hauptgang* *Entenbrust*
J: Oh, I'm trying to keep fit so I'd like something a bit lighter. Perhaps the *stuffed trout.*	*gefüllte Forelle*

TEST 3: English for dinner

Die ersten Buchstaben haben wir Ihnen gegeben.

Herr Ober! Ich hätte gerne die Speisekarte.	Excuse me, w________, could I have the menu, please?
Haben Sie schon gewählt?	Are you ready to o________?
Womit wollen Sie anfangen?	What would you like to s________ with?
Ich nehme die Suppe.	I'll t________ the soup.
Und danach?	And to f________?
Ich versuche mal das Lamm.	I'll t________ the lamb.
Was möchten Sie trinken?	What would you l________ to drink?
Ein kleines Helles.	A half of l________, please.
Ich möchte bitte zahlen.	Could I have the b________, please?

B: Okay, I'd *suggest* we try the dry Riesling. It's especially good with trout. — *vorschlagen*

J: That *sounds* like a good idea. — *sich anhören*

The evening *passed* quickly, and soon it was time to *leave*. — *vergehen*, *aufbrechen*

B: Excuse me, miss. Could I have the *bill*, please? — *Rechnung*

W: Yes sir, *straight away.* — *sofort*

J: Oh, you shouldn't Bernd. Let's *go Dutch*. That'd be fair. — *getrennt zahlen*

B: Okay, Jenny. That's nice of you. Listen. I wanted to tell you. You know I feel really good when we're together. Perhaps we could see each other again.

J: Well, I like being with you, too, but we've only known each other a week or so. And don't forget your friend Heidi. We still have to find her and quickly. And what then?

TEST 4: Noch einmal: Adjektiv oder Adverb?

1. He sleeps *good / well* that night.
2. He has a *good / well* night's sleep.
3. Bernd is *eager / eagerly* to see Jenny again.
4. He *eager / eagerly* looks forward to his date.
5. He feels really *good / well* when he is with Jenny.
6. I thinks the breast of duck sounds *good / well.*

TEST 5: Sprachfallen: *eventual* heißt nicht *eventuell*

possible • eventual • eventually

1. We have made a plan in order to avoid[1] ____________ difficulties.
2. She ____________ passed her driving test.
3. Our ____________ aim is to find a drug against cancer[2].
4. My company will ____________ use your service very often.

1 vermeiden 2 Krebs

17 kidnapped

Well, if we look back to the beginning of our story we'll find a "happy" *couple* coming to England on holiday. Then things began to go wrong. *As you remember* Heidi was in her hotel room without Bernd but with a suitcase that certainly *belonged* to somebody else. Then she was *sprayed* with something and *collapsed* on the floor. In the week that followed Bernd did his best to find her. He was assisted by Miss Mable, a *local* amateur private detective. The police had a photograph of Heidi but nothing has been heard *since*. So what exactly had happened in the middle of that night? Well, it *ran* more or less like this.
Heidi had opened the door to her room in the early hours of the morning. She didn't have the chance to see her *unexpected* visitor. Everything was *spinning* in front of here eyes. She fell to the ground.

Paar
wie Sie sich erinnern
gehören
besprühen
zusammenbrechen
ortsansässig
seitdem
sich ereignen
unerwartet; sich drehen

Auf einen BLICK

Schwerpunkt	Beispiel
1. Bedingungssätze	*If* you ask him he will help you.
2. wenn; seit	*if* oder *when, for* oder *since*?

TEST 1: Deutsch: *wenn* – Englisch: *if* oder *when*?

1. Tact is the art of saying nothing ______ there is nothing to say.
2. ______ you look like your passport photo you really need the holiday.
3. Why does a Lada have heated rear windscreens[1]?
   To keep your hands warm ______ you push it.
4. Don't tell lies ______ you can use statistics.
5. My wife says she'll leave me, ______ I don't throw out my computer.
   I'll miss her.

1 geheizte Rückscheibe

A shabby looking fellow *pushed into* the room. It didn't look good for the young woman. Sam Black, for that was his name, was *born* and *bred* in the *docklands* of London. Now and again he worked on the boats that fished *off* the coast of southern England. Sam was indeed a *fishy* character. This time he was involved with a *well-to-do* country gentleman who called himself Captain Reed. The Captain had a plan to get *a pile of money*. He was being helped by a young fellow, *apparently* his *nephew*, Blake, a good-looking *sun-tanned* man with laughing eyes.
Anyhow, Sam was in the hotel room. He looked around quickly. It didn't take a minute till he saw what he was looking for. The *flashy, posh* suitcase. "Got you at last, my *precious*. Got away from me at the hospital, didn't you, but not for long. If I *lose* you again the Captain will *stick* my feet into a *block of concrete* and throw me into the River Thames.

sich drängen

geboren; aufgewachsen; Hafenviertel; vor
verdächtig
wohlhabend

ein Haufen Geld
offensichtlich; Neffe; braungebrannt

protzig; pikfein
mein Schatz
verlieren
stecken; Betonklotz

TEST 2: *for* oder *since*?

1. Nothing has been heard of Heidi _______ she was kidnapped.
2. Patient: Aren't these pills habit-forming[1]?
Doctor: Rubbish, I've been taking them _______ years.
3. I have been in love with the same woman _______ forty years. If my wife finds out she'll kill me.

TEST 3: Es muss nicht immer *Present Perfect* sein

Ergänzen und übersetzen Sie.

1. We (*be married*) successfully (*seit*) four years. Then my wife (*lose*) her job.
2. I (*not be*) so upset[2] seit Margaret (*ask*) me what I wanted to name the baby. Margaret – that's my secretary.

1 süchtig machen 2 schockiert

17 Sam ran over to the brown suitcase and *pulled it apart.* "Aha! Yes, indeed. The three bags of *goodies* are still there. If she knew what that lot was *worth* she would be in the Bahamas by now." But *anyway* he was a bit confused. "What am I going to do with this woman? If I leave her here, the police will certainly get information from her. Did she see my face? I can't *take the risk.* What will the Captain say if I bring her back to the *safe house*? Damn me, I'm certainly *in a pickle* with all this.
He hears a noise downstairs. "Jesus, *someone's about.* Right." Sam throws the half-naked Heidi onto the bed, rolls her up in a *blanket* like a Chinese *spring roll* and *hoists* her over his shoulder.

aufreißen
tolle Sachen
wert
hier: dennoch
das Risiko eingehen
Versteck; in der Klemme
Da ist jemand
Decke; Frühlingsrolle; hieven

TEST 4: If-Sätze Typ I – Wie steht's mit den Verbformen?

1. If we *look* back to the beginning of the book we (*find*) a "happy" couple coming to England on holiday.
2. If Black (*lose*) the bag again the Captain *will stick* his feet into a block of concrete.
3. If Black *leaves* Heidi there, the police (*get*) information from her.
4. What (*say*) the Captain if he *brings* the girl to the safe house?

TEST 5: Können Sie steigern?

1. Suppliers are coming (*immer früher*).
2. The kidnapping ran (*mehr oder weniger*) like this.
3. Bernd did (*sein Bestes*) to find Heidi.

TEST 6: Setzen Sie ins Passiv

1. Black sprayed Heidi with something.
2. Black kidnapped Heidi.
3. Miss Mable assisted Bernd.
4. His nephew was helping the Captain.

Swindler (**S**) appears behind the reception desk. Sam Black (**B**) *freezes*. — *erstarren*

S: Oho, what are you doing in my hotel? It's five thirty in the morning. (Swindler *gazes* at Sam and the parcel on his shoulder). Aha, you're a *supplier*. You fellows are getting *earlier and earlier*. There was a time when people came at a civilised hour. *Nowadays* guests come at three in the morning, suppliers at five. No respect for anyone.

B: Well, sorry, *governor*. I wanted to make an early start. Excuse me, I'm sure. If it's okay with you I'll *be off* as quickly as I can.

S: Okay, okay. Good-bye and don't come so early next time. (To himself: In the old days we carried potatoes in *brown bags*, not in these white *fancy* cloth things. Hmmm. Times have changed.)

starren — gazes
Lieferant — supplier
immer früher — earlier and earlier
heutzutage — nowadays
Chef — governor
weg sein — be off
Papiertüten; fein — brown bags; fancy

TEST 7: If-Sätze Typ II – Wie steht's mit den Verbformen?

1. If Heidi (*know*) what was in the bag she *would be* in the Bahamas by now.
2. If Black (*lose*) the bag again the Captain *would stick* his feet into a block of concrete.
3. If Black (*leave*) her there, the police (*get*) information from her.

TEST 8: If-Sätze: Typ I und Typ II

1. Mum: Dad, please take Jimmy to the zoo today.
   Dad: Not me! (*Wenn der Zoo ihn will*), they can come and get him!
2. More husbands would leave home if (*wenn sie wüssten*) how to pack their suitcases.
3. Doctor: If I find it necessary to operate, (*werden Sie in der Lage sein [be able]*) to pay for it?
   Patient: (*Wenn ich das Geld nicht hätte*), *would* you find it necessary to operate?

18 in the lion's den[1]

Well, that *was a close shave* for slippery Sam, but only because Swindler is actually a *dumbo*. If he had only used his eyes he would have noticed it was one of his own *bed sheets*. In the meanwhile Sam *piled* Heidi into his *truck* and transported her to the *safe house* at 14 Castle road, Dover. Sam (**S**) *banged* on the door. Blake (**B**), the *handsome*, opened it.	*beinahe ins Auge gehen; Trottel* *Bettlaken; laden* *Lieferwagen; Versteck; hämmern* *fesch*
B: Where the devil have you been *hiding*? If you hadn't arrived in the next half hour we would have driven to your *place* to find you.	*sich verstecken* *Haus*
S: Well, I had a few problems, didn't I? Let me in, will you?	
B: Have you got the bags? What's that *carpet* over your shoulder?	*Teppich*
S: *It ain't* a carpet.	*It isn't (slang)*
By now they had entered a dark *living room* with a fire spluttering in the *fireplace*. A *pleasant-looking* country gentleman was sitting at a *low* wooden table. He was *enjoying* a double malt whisky. Captain Reed (**C**) looked up. He *smiled sweetly*.	*Wohnzimmer* *Kamin; freundlich* *niedrig* *genießen* *hold lächeln*

Auf einen BLICK

Schwerpunkt	Beispiel
1. Bedingungssätze Typ III	If I *had known* I'd *have told* you.
2. Will-Future Progressive	She'*ll be talking* to the police.

TEST 1: Wechseln Sie die Wortart

He said it with a sweet *smile.*	He said it and smiled ________.
He said it with a *dangerous* smile.	He smiled ________.
It's *probable* that she's seen you.	She's ________ seen you.
Sam did it with *extreme care.*	Sam did it ________ ________.

1 In der Höhle des Löwen

S: Sorry, *governor*. Look, there was an *emergency*. I *dislocated* my shoulder getting out of my truck. It was so *painful*. I had to go straight to *out-patients* at the hospital. They *put it back in joint*.	*Chef; Notfall ausrenken schmerzhaft; Ambulanz; einrenken*
C: Well, I'm sure we're all glad that you've *recovered your health*. So, *all's well that ends well*, as they say.	*wieder gesund werden; Ende gut, alles gut*
S: If it had all been so simple, that would have been great.	
C: Come on! *Spit it out*, man! Get to the point. (The captain smiled *dangerously*.)	*Spuck's aus gefährlich*
S: Well, sir. There was a *mix-up* at the hospital.	*Verwechslung*
C: Mix-up? Did they put the wrong shoulder into joint?	
S: No, sir. A young woman took my suitcase *by mistake*. With all the *sparklers*.	*aus Versehen Klunker*
The already dark living-room seemed to get *even darker*. The fire in the grate *died down* a little. The Captain *leaned back* in his seat.	*noch dunkler verlöschen zurücklehnen*

TEST 2: Welches ist das passende *Question Tag*?

1. Let me in, **A.** will you? / **B.** don't you?
2. Let's talk about it, **A.** will we? **B.** shall we?
3. He stole the bag while she was out, **A.** wasn't she? **B.** didn't he?
4. I'm stupid, **A.** am I not? / **B.** aren't I?
5. We'll have to kill the girl, **A.** won't we? / **B.** haven't we?

TEST 3: Wie steht es mit den kleinen Wörtern?

1. A girl picked ______ my suitcase.
2. She took the suitcase ______ mistake.
3. I managed to get hold ______ her address.
4. Get ______ the point, Sam.
5. I'm intrigued how you pulled it ______.
6. Now Blake spoke ______.

C: Sam, are you trying to tell me that you've lost the diamonds? If I had known there were going to be complications, I would never have sent you to get the suitcase.	
S: Governor, this girl *picked up* my suitcase and left the hospital with it.	*(mit-) nehmen*
C: *Well?*	*Na und?*
S: Well, I managed to *get hold of* her address, the hotel where she's staying. And I got the diamonds back again.	*bekommen*
C: You *stole* them *while* she was out, did you?	*stehlen; während*
S: Not exactly. She was in the room.	
C: In the room?	
S: Right.	
C: I must say I'm *intrigued* how you *pulled* it *off*. Where are the diamonds? Where's the girl?	*neugierig; es deichseln / schaffen*
Sam *fetched* the suitcase from the hall and *stood* it next to the table. He laid down the "*spring roll*" in the middle of the room and unrolled it. The captain lost his smile for the first time. He took another *swig* of his whisky.	*holen; stellen* / *Frühlingsrolle* / *Schluck*

TEST 4: Verbformen im Bedingungssatz Typ III

1. If Sam (*not arrive*), the Captain *would have driven* to his place.
2. If I *had known* the complications, I (*not send*) you.
3. If Christopher Columbus (*not discover*) America, he *would have saved* us a lot of trouble.
4. If Goethe *had used* a computer he (*may erase* [löschen]) Faust.

TEST 5: Was bedeutet das einfache *Will-Future*?

A. Voraussage B. Vermutung, Annahme C. Versprechen

1. The police *will force* her to talk. A
2. Well, we *will have to* kill her, won't we?
3. I'm sure she *won't tell* them anything.
4. Don't worry. Let me handle it. I *will take care* of her.

C: So, you've brought the girl here. She's probably seen you. She'll see all of us at the house. And *sooner or later* she'll be talking to the police. *What the hell* were you thinking of? | *früher; später* | *Was zum Teufel*

Blake was *as surprised as* the Captain at the situation, but looking at Heidi's pale face, he felt *sympathy* for her. And *by the way*, she was an attractive creature with her *bright* red hair. | *genauso überrascht wie; Mitleid; übrigens* | *leuchtend*

B: Oh, I'm sure she won't tell them anything. She's probably not the *sort.* | *Typ*

C: Probably not the sort? What sort? What's got into your head? They'll get to her. They'll *force* her. And why should she want to help us? We've got half a million pounds of diamonds in that suitcase. | *zwingen*

B: Well, I just thought ...

C: (interrupting) Thought. Think. Neither of you two have *a clue.* If I'd known that such a stupid thing could happen, I would never have *brought* you two *into my plans.* He took another swig. We'll have to kill her. *You realize that, don't you*? | *Ahnung* | *einweihen* | *Das ist euch klar, oder?*

TEST 6: Was bedeutet das *Will-Future Progressive*?

A. Höflichkeit B. nicht abgeschlossene Situation in der Zukunft
C. geplante oder automatische Folgehandlung

1. And sooner or later Heidi *will be talking* to the police. C
2. *Will you be staying* another night, sir?
3. Let me post this letter for you. On my way home I'*ll be passing* the post office anyway.
4. When you read this picture postcard I'll be lying on the beach in Florida.
5. *Will* you still *be sending* me Valentines when I'm sixty-four?
6. *Will* you *be paying* by credit card?

19 every cloud has a silver lining[1]

To tell the *truth* Blake was shocked. This whole adventure was *rapidly* becoming too hot for him. It was one thing to help someone *delivering* a few diamonds and *quite another* to kidnap and kill people. More than that, he didn't feel good with the Captain and Sam. Indeed the Captain had *explained* to him that he was getting back diamonds which had been in his *possession* earlier. The Captain spoke again.

Wahrheit
schnell
(ab-)liefern
etwas ganz anderes
erklären
Besitz

C: Okay, Sam. Put our *hostage* in the back bedroom and *lock* the door. Then you and me will drive to Canterbury. We have *a couple* of things to do. Blake, *take care of* our prisoner. We'll *deal with her* at the weekend.

Geisel
abschließen
ein paar
sich kümmern um

The Captain smiled *pleasantly* and told the two men that he had an *acquaintance* in Canterbury who specialised in *getting rid of* unwanted *baggage* of any sort. Five minutes later the front door *slammed* and Blake was *on his own.*

freundlich
Bekannte(r)
los werden; Ballast
zuknallen
allein

Auf einen BLICK

Schwerpunkt	Beispiel
Die Indirekte Rede	He *said* he *was* ill.

Die indirekte Rede – Daumenregel

Ist das einleitende Verb in einer Zeit der Vergangenheit, steht im Folgesatz ebenso eine Zeit der Vergangenheit.

Did you hear about the Irish tourist who paid £10 for a sheet of sandpaper[2]? He *thought* it *was* a map of the Sahara Desert.

1 Nach Regen kommt Sonnenschein 2 Bogen Sandpapier

Blake sat *glumly* in front of the fire. He thought he	*bedrückt*
had known what he *was getting into.* He put several	*sich einlassen auf*
logs on the fire. There was a bang from the bedroom	*Holzscheit*
next door. The girl was awake. Blake *rose,* walked over	*sich erheben*
to the door and *unlocked* it. Inside the dark room he	*aufsperren*
could see that Heidi had *rolled over* and fallen onto	*sich umdrehen*
the floor. She was half-naked. Blake decided that he	
should do something about the situation. He *fetched*	*holen*
his jacket and a knife, *untied* Heidi's hand and put	*losbinden*
the jacket around her shoulders.	
H: Where am I? What are you doing? Who are you	
anyway? My God, my head is *aching.*	*wehtun*
B: Look, I'm not going to *hurt* you, but you have to	*jemandem weh-*
be careful. He said he was going to kill you.	*tun*
H: Kill me? Why? I'm just a tourist.	
B: Let's go over to the fire. You can drink a *drop* of	*Tropfen*
something strong. It'll help. What can you *re-*	*sich erinnern*
member about the whole situation?	
Heidi didn't know what to think. This *pleasant* young	*freundlich*
man *obviously* wanted to help her, at least didn't	*offensichtlich*
want to *harm* her. She began to feel safer.	*schaden*

TEST 1: Indirekte Rede: Korrigieren Sie die Fehler

1. Tina thought Robinson Crusoe is a world famous tenor.
2. The first time Tina ever saw a cow she thought it is a bull that has swallowed a glove.
3. Bob told the mechanic to fill up the petrol tank. He thought that will double the price of his Trabi.

TEST 2: Übersetzen Sie die deutschen Klammern

1. The Captain told the men that (*er habe*) a friend in Canterbury.
2. He said (*er habe vor*) to kill Heidi.
3. Blake thought (*er wüsste*) what he was getting into.

19 Heidi *sipped* the whisky. It burned her *throat pleasantly.* "I don't remember much." He had asked her to *describe* what had happened. She *thought hard.*

nippen an; Kehle angenehm; beschreiben; angestrengt nachdenken

H: I was asleep. I think it was about five o'clock in the morning. My God! Now I remember. There were *bags* of diamonds in a suitcase. Somebody else's suitcase.

Beutel

B: That's right. The Captain said he had *recovered* them from an old friend who had stolen them from him.

wiederbeschaffen

Heidi told Blake that she had *apparently* picked up the wrong suitcase *by accident* at the hospital. She went on to explain how somebody had *sprayed* some sort of gas into her face.

offenbar; aus Versehen; sprühen

B: That was Sam. He's dangerous. I don't *trust* him. He didn't know what to do with you, so he *bundled you up* in a blanket and brought you here. By the way, you aren't *hurt*, are you?

vertrauen; verpacken; verletzt

H: My head aches and my eyes are *sore*, but *apart from* that I'm okay. So, you're a gang of three? What's your role in all this?

entzündet; abgesehen davon

TEST 3: Entscheiden Sie: Adjektiv oder Adverb?

1. Blake didn't feel *happy / happily* with the Captain and Sam.
2. The two talked and talked and got on *good / well* together.
3. The Captain smiled *pleasant / pleasantly.*
4. The *pleasant / pleasantly* young Blake wanted to help Heidi.

TEST 4: Was ist gemeint?

1. Blake *takes care of* the prisoner. **A.** sorgen für **B.** bewachen
2. Blake went to *look after* Heidi. **A.** sehen nach **B.** suchen
3. The Captain will *deal with* her. **A.** töten **B.** verhandeln

B: I think I've been naïve. The Captain told me I could *earn* a bit of extra money to *support* my university course.	*verdienen; unterstützen / finanzieren*
The two talked and talked and got on well together. Heidi also felt attracted to this young man. She asked Blake why they *both* simply should not run away to the police.	*beide*
B: Listen, Heidi, it's too *dangerous*. If the police don't catch the Captain, he'll follow us and find us. And he'll kill us. I think the diamonds *are worth a lot.*	*gefährlich; viel wert sein*
H: Maybe. And there's your *part* in all this. I'm not sure what would happen to you.	*Rolle*
B: Listen, the Captain told me he would deal with you at the weekend. Perhaps we could make some *careful* plans in the next two days. Then we could both *disappear* on the Friday. In such a way that nobody can find us *till all this has blown over.*	*sorgfältig; verschwinden; bis Gras darüber gewachsen ist*
H: We won't have much chance to talk, though.	
B: Yes, we will. The Captain and Sam both have a lot of things to arrange outside the house. They wanted to *be gone* by Sunday. Listen, just trust me! I'll have *to tie you up* again. They mustn't *suspect* anything.	*verschwinden; fesseln; argwöhnen*

TEST 5: Blake berichtet, was man ihm erzählt hat

1. "You can earn a bit of extra money."
   The Captain *told* me (that) ______________________________
2. "I am getting back my diamonds."
   He explained (that) ______________________________
3. "I'll deal with the girl at the weekend."
   He told me (that) ______________________________
4. Heidi: "I picked up the wrong suitcase."
   Heidi told me (that) ______________________________

20 back on the trail

Meanwhile back in Hastings Miss Mable was sitting together with Bernd discussing strategy. They were *enjoying* afternoon coffee and tea at Holiday Out. Well, *you need*n't *expect* a good cup of coffee in Hastings. The best you'll get is *lukewarm liquid*. People often don't even know if they are drinking coffee or tea. *Speaking* of the tea – well, Mr Swindler always uses one *teabag* for two people. "Waste not, want not," as he's *fond of* saying.	inzwischen; genießen; man braucht; erwarten; lauwarme Flüssigkeit; à propos; Teebeutel; gerne sagen
M: I'*m* very *keen on* visiting Inspector Reed's address in Dover. I'm interested in meeting the charming gentleman. Do you have time tomorrow, or *are you entertaining*? (Miss Mable had a *knowing* smile on her face.)	scharf sein auf; Gäste haben; wissend
B: Of course not. I'm *available* at any time.	verfügbar
M: Good, then let's go *as soon as possible*. It might be important. Let's *set off* first thing in the morning.	so schnell wie möglich; aufbrechen
B: That's fine with me. Whenever you're *ready*.	bereit

Auf einen BLICK

Schwerpunkte	Beispiel
1. Das Gerund – eine *ing*-Form	I'm keen on *visiting* Mr Reed.
2. Sprachfallen	*use* something, (be) *used to*

Das Gerund kann mehrere Funktionen im Satz haben:	
Subjekt	*Planning* means replacing chance by error.
Objekt	Credit cards have made *buying* easier but *paying* harder.
Prädikat	The hardest thing about boxing *is picking* up your teeth with a boxing glove on.

	(Miss Mable *stuck* her *fork* into a doughnut. Pieces *broke off* the *rocky* material).	*stecken; Gabel abbrechen; steinig; tun müssen*
M:	You see, Bernd. You *need to do* everything at the right time. Waiting can be *disastrous*, as you see *from the example of* Swindler's dead doughnuts. Let's hope it's not a bad *omen.*	*verheerend am Beispiel von Vorzeichen*
	(Bernd was beginning to get nervous.)	
B:	Perhaps we shouldn't wait at all. Let's go now.	

At that moment Swindler's ears *pricked up.* He had been cleaning a table nearby. — *hellhörig werden*

S:	Just a moment! *Slipping off* and hoping I wouldn't *notice,* perhaps.	*verschwinden bemerken*
M:	I do beg your pardon, Mr Swindler. I'm sure you have *misunderstood* our intentions.	*missverstehen*
S:	Perhaps, Miss Mable, but I can't risk *losing* money when *customers* forget to pay. *Especially* our older customers.	*verlieren Kunde; besonders*
M:	Good gracious me. *How dare you*? Mr Swindler, if I were three months younger, I would *warm your ear* with my umbrella. Put these teas on my bill and let's hear no more of this. Bernd, let's go to the *railway station.*	*Wie können Sie es wagen?; eins auf die Ohren geben Bahnhof*

TEST 1: Das Gerund steht nach Präpositionen

Übersetzen Sie die Ausdrücke in Klammern.

1. Miss Mable is (*scharf darauf zu besuchen*) Inspector Reed.
2. She is (daran interessiert zu treffen) the inspector.
3. They have (*Schwierigkeiten einzubrechen in*) Reed's house.
4. Tact is the (*Kunst zu sagen*) nothing when there is nothing to say.

TEST 2: Haben Sie Sprachgefühl? Gerund oder Infinitiv?

1. You needn't (*expect*) a good cup of coffee in Hastings.
2. I can't risk (*lose*) money when customers forget to pay.
3. They took a taxi to avoid (*arrive*) in the dark.
4. The first man (*tear*) a telephone book probably had teenage kids.

20 They arrived in Dover in the late afternoon and took a taxi to Castle Road to *avoid* arriving in the dark. Number fourteen was a Victorian *terraced house* with four levels including a *basement.* Miss Mable was *disappointed.*

M: Do you see any *light* at all? I don't. I'm afraid we'll have *difficulty* in getting into this place.
B: Getting in? You don't mean to *break into* someone else's *property*, do you?
M: Not really, but *there's no knowing* what we might find. Anyway, the inspector has some sort of *truck.*
B: How do you know that? There's no *vehicle* on the street.
M: Perfectly correct, my friend, but please *notice* the two *pools* of diesel oil next to the *curb.* Somebody has parked here regularly. You can even see the *tyre print* in that *mud* there. Now, I'll just knock at the door. (She bangs on the door with her umbrella.)

vermeiden
Reihenhaus
Keller
enttäuscht
Licht
Schwierigkeit
einbrechen
Grundstück
man kann nie wissen; Lieferwagen; Fahrzeug
bemerken
Pfütze; Randstein
Reifenabdruck
Matsch

TEST 3: Sprachfalle *use*

Welche Übersetzung passt?

A. verwenden
B. früher (etwas getan haben)
C. sich gewöhnen an
D. Es hat keinen Zweck

1. As a boy Bernd *used to climb* trees and fences. B
2. But he is not *used to breaking* into someone else's house.
3. Mr Swindler always *uses* one *teabag* for two people.
4. I *used to be* a werewolf, but I'm alright noooooow.
5. I *used to be* arrogant. Now I'm perfectly okay.
6. It's no *use crying* over spilled milk.

M: Bernd, please try to get around the *back* over that *fence* and see if you can find anything. I'll look down in the *basement*.	*Rückseite* *Zaun* *Keller*
Bernd *struggled over* the fence and broke a wooden *plank* off by accident. "I'm not *used to* climbing around strange houses," he *moaned* to himself. At the back there was almost no garden, just a *yard*. All the windows had *blinds* and they were all *pulled down*. "A complete *waste of time*." Bernd started climbing back over the fence. He was *just in time* to see Miss Mable climbing the *stairs* from the basement with some difficulty. Next minute everything seemed to happen so quickly and loudly. *Round the corner* a police car *came racing up with its siren shrieking*. Bernd tried to jump down from the fence, got his trousers *caught on* a *nail* and he fell off.	*mühsam klettern* *Brett; gewohnt an* *stöhnen* *Hof* *Jalousien; herunterlassen; Zeitverschwendung; gerade rechtzeitig* *Treppe* *um die Ecke* *heranrasen; mit heulender Sirene* *an einem Nagel hängen bleiben*
Miss Mable *stopped dead*. Two officers jumped out of the car. "*Lost your way*, you two, have you?"	*erstarren; sich verlaufen*

TEST 4: Infinitiv oder Gerund? Richtig oder Falsch?

	R	F
1. The art of medicine consists in amusing the patient while nature cures the disease[1].		
2. My way to joke is to tell the truth.		
3. Psychiatrist: Do you have difficulty in making up your mind[2]? Patient: Well, yes and no.		
4. A diplomat is a man who can tell you to go to hell in such a way that you actually look forward to go on the trip.		
5. Clarity is the ability to give directions[3] without taking your hands out of your pockets.		

1 Krankheit 2 sich entscheiden 3 Anweisungen geben

21 the police – our best friends

Well, what a *stupid* situation! If two people had ever looked *sheepish* it was Miss Mable and her young assistant Bernd. Policeman (**P**)

P: Could you two please come out of there *immediately*? You, young man! *Was* it *worth* ruining your clothes for? I wish to see some form of *identity*. I see you tried to climb the fence and, of course, you've broken it. That's *malicious damage*. Unless you have a plausible explanation to offer. And you, madam. Aren't you a bit old for this sort of thing?

M: Well, really! Excuse me, constable; *it isn't what it looks like*. If you'll allow me to explain.

Just then the other policeman came back from the house. "There's nobody at home. So, I think we'd like to *invite* you two to *accompany* us to the police station. *If you please*, into the car."
Ten minutes later our two *burglars* were sitting in the *interview room* with the police sergeant.

dumm
dämlich
sofort
sich lohnen
Ausweispapier
vorsätzliche Beschädigung
es ist nicht so, wie es scheint
einladen; begleiten
darf ich bitten?
Einbrecher
Verhörzimmer

Auf einen BLICK

Schwerpunkt	Beispiel
1. Bernds Personalien	What's your permanent address?
2. Infinitiv oder Gerund	Allow me *to explain.*

TEST 1: Was Polizisten so fragen

1. In welchem Hotel wohnen Sie?	______
2. Seit wann sind Sie in England?	______
3. Wann sind Sie geboren?	______
4. Wo sind Sie geboren?	______
5. Wo ist Ihr ständiger Wohnsitz?	______

This *guardian* of law and order *intended* to *get* to the *bottom* of the whole *issue*. Sergeant (**S**). — *Hüter; wollen Grund; Sache*

S: You first, sir. Could I have your name and address, please?

B: Bubel. Bernd Bubel. I'm from Germany.

S: What's your exact address, please?

B: Heidelberg, Bergheimer Straße 52.

S: Okay. Could you give me the number of the house, the street, the city and the *postal code* in that order, please? — *Postleitzahl*

Bernd did as he was told. He was frustrated. He hadn't known he needed to give the number of the house first. The sergeant warned him not to leave the area *until* everything was *sorted out*. Next the sergeant *decided* to interview Miss Mable who had been getting more and more nervous. "I wish you would allow me to explain the *circumstances*." — *bis (auf)klären; beschließen* — *Umstände*

S: *Everything in good time.* If you please, name and *residence*. — *alles zu seiner Zeit; Wohnsitz*

M: Edith Mable, and my *permanent address* is in Bournemouth, 6 Sea View. — *ständiger Wohnsitz*

TEST 2: Wie steht es im Ausweis?

Nehmen Sie Ihren Personalausweis und ergänzen Sie.

_ _ _ _ of _ _ _ _ _ :	08.03.1977
P _ _ _ _ of _ _ _ _ _:	Heidelberg
N_ _ _ _ _ _ _ _ _ _ _:	German
R_ s _ d _nc _:	Heidelberg
C_ _ _ _ _ of _ _ _ _	blue
Signature of b _ _ _ _ _ :	Bernd Bubel
H_ _ _ _ _ :	182 cm

S: Miss Mable? You're not *by any chance* the *famous* Miss Mable, the amateur detective and *novelist*, are you?
M: I do have that *honour*, yes.
S: Oh, I see. Well, Miss Mable, *what was it all about*?

zufällig; berühmt
Romanschrift-steller(in)
Ehre
um was ging es?

The old lady gave a short *summary* of the week's *events*. Finally she explained that she thought she had heard somebody at the *terraced house* in Dover just before the police arrived. The sergeant, who was a fan of Miss Mable's work, was *pacified* by the story.

Zusammenfassung
Ereignisse
Reihenhaus
besänftigt

S: Well, of course, you shouldn't have been in the garden, but it was *in a good cause*, I *suppose*.
M: Sergeant, you know all your colleagues and *staff*. Does the name Inspector Reed mean anything to you?
S: He certainly doesn't work for the force in East Sussex or Kent. I can tell you that.

zu einem guten Zweck; vermuten
Personal

The sergeant *offered* to drive *the odd couple* back to their hotel. Miss Mable *accepted* but asked the policeman to *drop* them *off* at the nearest post-office for a minute or two.

anbieten; das ungleiche Paar
annehmen; absetzen

TEST 3: Richtig oder falsch – Infinitiv oder Gerund?

R F

1. Then the sergeant decides interviewing Bernd.
2. Bernd denies stealing anything.
3. He doesn't risk to tell lies to the sergeant.
4. Was it worth to ruin his clothes for?
5. Miss Mable says she has come to visit her nephew.
6. But he doesn't appear living there any more.
7. Perhaps the postman can help you to find him.

Fortunately the post-office was still open and the young lady (**L**) behind the *counter* seemed to be a bit *bored.* | *zum Glück; Schalter; gelangweilt*

L: *How can I be of assistance?* | *Was kann ich für Sie tun?*
M: Thank you very much. Well, I'd like five first class stamps and five envelopes, please.
L: Yes, that'll be two pounds fifty pence.
M: Right. You're a *local* girl, aren't you? It's a lovely part of the world down here, isn't it? | *hiesig / von hier*
L: Yes, I'm from the old town.
M: Are you *indeed*? I've come to visit my nephew, but he doesn't *appear* to live here any more. His house is *empty.* What *a waste of a journey*! | *wirklich; scheinen; leer; vergebliche Reise*
L: Hmmm. *Perhaps* I can help you to find him. What's the address, did you say? | *vielleicht*
M: 14, Castle Road, Dover.
L: Yes, they have left a *forwarding address.* | *Nachsendeadresse*
M: Was it Inspector Reed?
L: Captain Reed, actually. 6 The Mews, Brighton.

TEST 4: Nicht verwechseln – *near, nearest, next, nearby*

1. Miss Mable asked the policeman to drop them off at (*dem nächsten*) post-office.
2. "How come you were born in Iowa?" – "I wanted to be (*in der Nähe von*) my mother."
3. Mike was asked what his favourite drink was. "The (*nächste*) one," he replied.
4. Excuse me, where is (*die nächste*) toilet? It's urgent.

TEST 5: Übersetzen Sie. Auf die Stellung kommt es an

1. He wanted to marry *her*.	Er wollte ________________
2. He wanted *her* to marry.	Er wollte ________________
3. He wanted *her* to marry him.	Er wollte ________________

22 thinking the day over

The Dover police, trying to be both *efficient* and friend-	*tüchtig*
ly, *bundled* Miss Mable and Bernd into a new police	*verpacken*
car and *sped* them across country to our friendly hotel	*rasen*
in Hastings. *By now* it was almost dark. You can ima-	*inzwischen*
gine a warm *dusk*, loving *couples strolling* around and	*Dämmerung; Paa*
then suddenly the police car arrives making a noise	*bummeln*
like a *car-chase* in a Hollywood film. The car *screeched*	*Verfolgungsjagd*
to a halt in front of Holiday Out. Policeman (**P**)	*mit quietschender Reifen anhalten*
P: Here you are, Miss. Home *safe and sound.*	*wohlbehalten*
M: Well, really! What were you thinking of? People will get the shock of their lives.	
The policeman *escorts* them through the front door of Holiday Out.	*begleiten*
B: I *suppose* Mr Swindler will be frustrated.	*annehmen*

Auf einen BLICK

Schwerpunkt	Beispiel
1. Unregelmäßige Verben	become, became, become
2. Verben mit Präpositionen etc.	tie someone *up*

TEST 1: Drei verschiedene Verben für *annehmen*

1. Miss Mable ______________ the policeman's offer.
2. Miss Mable ______________ the day's events have made Bernd nervous.
3. I ______________ Mr Swindler will be frustrated.

Time for a smile

A family arrived at Holiday Out.
"Do you take children?" the man asked Mr Swindler.
"No, sir," replied Swindler. "Only cash and credit cards."

S:	*Did I hear my name taken in vain?* Oh, I might have guessed it would be you two. You can't come to the hotel without bringing half of the East Sussex police force with you. Perhaps you do that sort of thing in your country, but around here people *use* buses.	*Wer lästert gerade über mich?* *benützen*
M:	It's all too complicated to explain.	
S:	Oh, yes of course. I'm too *stupid* to know about why my guests arrive in police cars *every second day.* Let's talk about the weather. That's certainly a simpler *subject.*	*dumm* *jeden zweiten Tag* *Thema*
M:	Mr Swindler. Please don't *throw* one of your *tantrums.* You'd be far more useful to us if you would be so kind as to bring us a *nightcap* in the lounge. Bernd, what may I offer you, a brandy?	*Wutanfälle bekommen* *Gutenachttrunk*
B:	Why not indeed? It's been a day to remember, or rather to forget.	
S:	Oh, has it really? Well, I'm *glad* somebody has something to *complain* about. You should try taking care of this hotel. It's like a *lunatic asylum.*	*froh* *sich beklagen* *Irrenhaus*

TEST 2: Setzen Sie in das *Simple Past*

1. The police car *speeds* them across country to Hastings.
2. Blake *hears* a voice outside.
3. He *blows* the candle out.
4. Swindler *throws* a tantrum.

Time for a smile

Swindler: I can offer you three days and two nights for £55.
Guest: How come so cheap?
Swindler: The days are July 11, 12 and 13.
The nights are July 21 and 22.

M: Thank you for that *illuminating* information, Mr Swindler. We were *wondering* about the drinks. Will we get them today or tomorrow, perhaps?	*aufschlussreich* *sich fragen*
S: Yes, and that's the next thing. Poor old Swindler, Hastings' specialist in *cream teas* and telepathy.	*Tee mit Marmeladekuchen und Sahne;*
Five minutes later our two *adventurers* are seated at a small table near the bar. Miss Mable is excited about something. Bernd *presumes* it is the day's *events*. "After all, it's not every day you *trespass* on other people's property and get *caught red-handed*."	*Abenteurer* *vermuten; Ereignisse; eindringen* *auf frischer Tat ertappt*
B: You're very *flustered* about our *bad luck* today, aren't you?	*aufgeregt; Pech*
M: Not *particularly*, my boy. No, actually I'm *worrying* about something else which is far more important.	*besonders; sich sorgen*
B: Financial problems?	
M: No, health problems!	
B: You don't feel well?	
M: Not my health. I was talking about Heidi.	
B: What do you mean by that?	

TEST 3: Je kürzer das Wort, desto schwieriger

1. Blake tied Heidi ______ again.
2. A car drove ______.
3. They trespassed ______ other people's property.
4. They were wondering ______ the drinks.
5. What were you thinking ______, Bernd?

Time for a smile

To understand Mr Swindler's character better you should know that he is so mean[1] that he steals towels from the guests.

1 geizig

M: Listen Bernd, *in spite of* what that *pushy* young policeman said at 14, Castle Road in Dover, I *believe* my own ears and my intuitions. I'm quite certain somebody was in the house who didn't want to see us. And now they *realise* we are after them. Heidi could be in real danger.

ungeachtet; aufdringlich
glauben
begreifen

So what exactly had happened back in 14, Castle Road? You will *remember* it was early evening. Blake and Heidi had just had their tête à tête about what to do for the best. They heard a *voice* outside. Blake was alarmed. "Jesus, quick, get in the bedroom. Let me *tie you up*. They're back already." Heidi was lying on the bed again. Blake could hear *movements* outside. Suddenly there was a loud knocking. He *blew* the *candle* out and sat down in the chair banging his knee on the table. The *shuffling* outside went on for five minutes and a few words were *exchanged*. Now Blake *recognised* a woman's voice. Suddenly there was a *screeching of tyres* and a police siren. "Jesus, we've been *discovered*," he *breathed*. In the next three or four minutes, which seemed to *last for ever*, there was more knocking and hammering on the door. Then a car door *slammed*, a car drove off and it became *silent* outside.

sich erinnern
Stimme
fesseln
Bewegung
blasen
Kerze
Schlurfen
austauschen
erkennen
Reifenquietschen
entdecken; hauchen; ewig dauern
zuknallen; still

TEST 4: In der Kürze liegt die Würze

Ersetzen Sie das *Kursivgedruckte* durch Infinitiv oder *-ing*-Form.

1. It's been a day *one should not forget.*
2. It's been a *day which is worth remembering.*
3. The police car arrived *and made* a terrible noise.
4. The police, *who were trying* to be friendly, bundled them into a police car.
5. Blake sat down in the chair *and banged* his knee on the table.

23

23 with his back to the wall

Blake waited for ten or fifteen minutes. It was still quiet. "Well, *the downside* is that somehow they've found out about us. *The upside* is that Heidi really has decided to come with me." Suddenly there was the sound of a key in the door. The Captain *strode* quickly into the sitting room *followed* by *evil-looking* Sam.

das Schlechte
das Gute
schreiten
gefolgt von; finster

C: You did well, Blake, to keep her *quiet*. That was the *cops* outside. I saw everything from the other end of the street.
B: They didn't realise there was anybody in here. We had no lights on.
C: We'll have to *bring forward* our plans. We'll leave tonight.
S: What about the girl? Shall I go and *do* her *in* now?

ruhig
Bullen
beschleunigen
kalt machen

Blake felt a *cold shiver run* down his back. He was *on his own* here. Sam was a nasty piece of work and Blake was sure the Captain had a gun in his *pocket*.

kalter Schauder
auf sich alleine gestellt; Hosentasche

Auf einen BLICK

	Schwerpunkt	Beispiel
1.	Wie übersetzt man *wie*?	*as, like* oder *how*?
2.	Nicht verwechseln!	*then* oder *than, quite* oder *quiet*

Notice in Swindler's lounge

The water in this hotel is completely hygienic.
It has all been passed[1] personally by Mr Swindler.

1 pass water ist zweideutig: a) Wasser lassen, b) Wasser prüfen

Sam began to walk *towards* the bedroom door. Blake stood up, his heart *pounding.* | *in Richtung auf; hämmern*

C: Wait a minute, Sam, we have to organise this *properly*, or we'll *give ourselves away.* We'll do this part as we planned – at the *quarry.* Listen, you fetch the truck, get it tanked up and ready. I'll phone Dick and tell him what's happened. After all, he's going to *get rid of* the *baggage*, so he'll need to bring his *concrete truck* along. | *ordentlich; sich verraten; Steinbruch; loswerden; Flittchen; Betonmischmaschine*

S: Okay, boss. Just as you like. I'll be away for at least an hour.

C: Do it all as quickly as you can. Blake, *clear up* here. Make sure there's nothing that *belongs* to us. Then *wipe over* everything with a *damp cloth.* And give this powder to the girl to drink. That'll keep her quiet. | *Klarschiff machen; gehören; abwischen; feuchtes Tuch*

B: Right you are, boss. When will you be back?

C: In about two hours, I hope. Then we can load up the girl, *pass* the quarry on the way and then *off to* Brighton. | *vorbeifahren; ab nach Brighton*

TEST 1: Wie übersetzt man *wie*?

1. Do it *as* quickly (*wie*) you can.
2. Blake's brain was working (*wie*) a whirlwind.
3. We'll do it (*wie*) planned.
4. (*Wie*) is the Captain?
5. (*Wie*) is the Captain like?

TEST 2: Nicht verwechseln! Übersetzen Sie!

Blake waited *for ten minutes.*	Blake ______________
Blake has waited *for ten minutes.*	Blake ______________.
How is Tom?	______________ Tom?
What is Tom like?	______________ Tom?

23 with his back to the wall

The door *slammed.* Blake waited until he heard the car and the truck drive off. He ran into the bedroom and *freed* Heidi. "They'll be back in an hour. They want me to *drug* you. Then they'll kill you. We have to act quickly. Let's make a plan."
The whisky was still on the table. They had a couple of glasses while they were planning. Heidi was glad of the *liquid.* She had begun to get quite cold. They *agreed* to go to London *till the coast was clear.* Blake had a couple of old friends there. Blake's hope was that the Captain would get his diamonds and then forget all about the two of them. He hadn't lost anything through Blake yet. He'd *prefer* to go *further away* than London, but travelling costs money. Then he heard the *noise* of the diesel truck.
"Sam's back half an hour *early.* Heidi quick, back in the bedroom."
Just then they heard Sam's key *turn* in the door.

zuknallen
befreien
betäuben
Flüssigkeit
sich einigen; bis die Luft rein ist
vorziehen; weiter weg
Geräusch
zu früh
sich drehen

TEST 3: Nicht verwechseln!

then • than • quite • quiet • somebody • anybody

1. Heidi began to get _________ cold.
2. The drug will keep Heidi _________.
3. _________ he heard the noise of the diesel truck.
4. Don't let your superiors know you're better _________ they are.
5. There was _________ in the house.
6. But the police thought there wasn't _________ in the house.

TEST 4: Erinnern Sie sich an den Wortlaut im Text?

1. the *positive aspect* of a situation	the _________ of a situation
2. the *negative aspect* of a situation	the _________ of a situation
3. *kill somone*	_________________
4. *tidy up* the house	_________ the house

S: I got finished quicker than I expected. And I thought I'd come back and help you with the girl *in case* you got cold feet.
B: Right you are! I was just starting to *tidy up* when I saw the Captain's malt whisky standing on the table. It's bloody good!
S: I bet it is. He's a gentleman, that man. He only drinks the best. I'll have a *drop* with you. Then we can *sort out* the woman.
B: I'll get us some glasses. We'd only have to throw the whole bottle away, anyway. *What a waste*!

Blake's active, *university-tuned* brain was working like a *whirlwind*. He picked up the bottle of the whisky, went to the *sideboard* where the Captain had left the *powder*. With his *back* between Sam and the whisky he *emptied* the powder into the glass and filled it with the yellow *liquid*.

für den Fall, dass
aufräumen
Tropfen
erledigen
Was für eine Verschwendung!
akademisch geschult; Wirbelwind; Büffet
Pulver; Rücken
(ent-)leeren
Flüssigkeit

TEST 5: Noch mal das Wörtchen *wie*

Drei Sätze sind falsch. Korrigieren Sie!

1. Blake felt *how* a cold *shiver runs* down his back.
2. Just then they heard *as* Sam's key turns in the door.
3. A woman who wants to be *as* a man has no ambition.
4. Etiquette is knowing *how* to yawn[1] with your mouth closed.

TEST 6: *our, us* oder *ourselves*?

1. Let _________ make a plan.
2. We'll have to bring forward _________ plans.
3. The downside is that they've found out about _________.
4. We have to organize this properly, or we'll give _________ away.

1 gähnen

24 24 on the run

They sat at the *low table* with two full glasses. Sam looked aggressive. — *Couchtisch*

S: You've not exactly had a lot to do on the trip, have you?
B: I've done my *part.* At least I haven't *put* the whole operation *in danger* like you have. — *Teil; in Gefahr bringen*
S: That could've happened to anybody.

They both took a *gulp* of the warming *liquid.* — *Schluck; Flüssigkeit; Tropfen*
S: Christ, that's a real *drop* of what does me good. The Captain'll be *barging in on* us soon. *Pour* me another! — *hereinplatzen; einschenken*
Which Blake did, almost with *pleasure.* — *Vergnügen*

S: Where will you be going after we leave the *safe house* in Brighton? — *Versteck*
B: Oh, I'm not sure about that yet. I'm going to stay with friends in Scotland. (Blake wanted to *lay* a *false trail* for Sam so they couldn't find him later.) — *falsche Spur legen*

S: Right, well, you'd better give me ...
Sam *groaned* and rolled over against the *arm* of the sofa. The *powder* had *done its job.* — *stöhnen; Lehne; Pulver; wirken*

Auf einen BLICK

	Schwerpunkt	Beispiel
1.	Die Formen des Futurs	*will do; will be doing; going to* do
2.	Wohin mit dem Adverb?	Heidi *boldly* walked in.

Time for a smile

Mr Swindler stared at the red-skinned guest and asked, "Do you have a reservation?" The guest answered, "Sure have, great big place near Rio Grande. How!"

Blake moved *like a flash of lightning*. He called Heidi into the room. "Here, put these jogging clothes on quickly. You're still half naked." Blake then sat Sam *upright*, put Blake's own glass next to his hand and *removed* Sam's glass and washed it. Blake carefully poured more of the whisky into Sam's mouth *spilling* some of it on his shirt.	*wie der Blitz* *aufrecht* *entfernen* *verschütten*
H: What are you doing that for? **B:** To *confuse* the Captain. Listen, we should get out now. Where's the suitcase? Aha!	*verwirren*
Blake pulled it open, looked at the *bags* for a second and *carefully* took two diamonds from each sack.	*Beutel* *vorsichtig*
H: Why don't you take more? **B:** The Captain will never *notice* these few stones. And it's a sort of *payment* anyway. It'll help us to go underground, just *in case*. (Blake *picked up the phone* and called a taxi.) "You can be here in three minutes. Fine. Please take us to Dover Bus	*bemerken* *Bezahlung* *für den Fall, dass;* *den Hörer abnehmen*

TEST 1: Bilden Sie die Verlaufsform des *Will-Future*

1. The Captain / barge in / on us soon.
2. Where / you go / after we leave Brighton?
3. you / stay/ long / or is it another flying visit?

Was drückt diese Form des Futurs in Beispiel 1 bzw. 2 und 3 aus?

TEST 2: Bilden Sie das *Going to-Future*

1. The Captain / barge in / on us soon.
2. Where / you go / after we leave Brighton?
3. you / stay/ long / or is it just a flying visit?

Was drückt diese Form des Futurs aus?

24 At Dover Bus Station they got out, waited until the taxi had left and jumped into another taxi. Then back to Dover Railway Station, where they had a cup of tea and a discussion. The problem was that Heidi had no *identity card*, no passport and no bank cards. Where was her original suitcase? She hadn't seen it since she had been at the hospital. *Fast-thinking* Blake quickly got the number of the *accident ward.* He passed the receiver to Heidi. Of course, it was Jenny who answered the phone. She *was on duty* again.

Ausweis
Schnelldenker
Unfallstation
Dienst haben

H: Hello. Is that the accident ward? I left my suitcase there a week ago and ...
J: Yes, I remember. *My goodness*, you're Heidi, aren't you? — *Mein Gott!*
H: Yes, eh no! I mean it's a long story. Where's the suitcase?
J: Bernd took it to his room in the Holiday Out. Hey, are you okay?
H: Yes, I'm fine. Eh, how did you remember Bernd's name?
J: That's a long story, too.
H: Okay. Could you tell him I'm fine. See you!

TEST 3: Bilden Sie das einfache *Will-Future*

1. It / be / about 8:30 *p.m.* when they arrive at the hotel.
2. The chances are that Bernd / not be / at the hotel.
3. The diamonds / help /our heroes to go underground.

Was drückt diese Form des Futurs aus?

TEST 4: Korrigieren Sie die Fehler

1. I left my suitcase a week ago at the accident ward.
2. Please bring us to Dover Bus Station.
3. Why are you doing that for?
4. Blake moved as a flash of lightning.

Blake thought for a minute. "Well, *there's no way around it*. We have to get into your room at Holiday Out. The chances are that Bernd will be somewhere else. It'll be about 8:30 *p.m.* when we arrive there."	*es gibt keinen anderen Weg*
On the train to Hastings they *hatched* their plan.	*ausbrüten*
Blake would phone the hotel to see if Bernd was in. Then Heidi would *boldly* walk in and ask for the key	*kühn*
to room six. *After all* it was her room. Heidi walked up	*immerhin*
to the reception desk in the hotel. She *tapped* the bell.	*tippen*
Swindler *popped up* from behind the desk.	*auftauchen*
S: Well, well, well! *Look what the cat's dragged in.* The guest *in transit*. I'm not the only one looking for you, you know.	*wen haben wir denn da?; auf der Durchreise*
H: I've been *indisposed* in the last few days.	*unpässlich*
S: Yes, *I bet* you have.	*ich wette*
H: Can I have my key?	
S: You certainly don't remember where your room is, do you? Will you be staying long, or is it another *flying visit*?	*Stippvisite*

TEST 5: Wohin mit dem Adverb?

carefully • quickly • certainly • boldly • really

1. Blake __________ poured __________ whisky into Sam's mouth.
2. Blake __________ got __________ the number of the ward.
3. Then Heidi __________ walked __________ into the hotel.
4. You _________ don't _________ remember where your room is, do you?
5. To err is human but to __________ foul __________ things up you need a computer.

TEST 6: Übersetzen Sie

1. Sam sat upright.
2. Blake sat Sam upright.
3. You'd better give me another whisky.
4. They had a cup of tea.

25 no requiem for Sam

Heidi *was in luck.* No Bernd. She couldn't possibly have explained everything to him in a hurry. She found her passport and bank cards. On the way out she paid Swindler what she still *owed* him. — *Glück haben*; *schulden*

S: My, oh my. She's had a *fit of conscience.* Suddenly wants to pay her bills. But still *popping in* and *popping out.* Does your boyfriend know about all this? — *Gewissensbiss*; *auftauchen; verschwinden*

H: No, it's all happened so quickly. I'll write him a letter.

S: Oh, that's good of you, I'm sure. People have *spent* a lot of *time* searching for you. You could have *left a message.* — *Zeit verbringen*; *Nachricht hinterlassen*

H: I was sort of *tied up.* Listen, I have to rush. Somebody's after me. — *verhindert (gefesselt)*

S: After you? That seems to be a normal *condition of life* with you. Good-bye. — *Lebensumstand*

Auf einen BLICK

	Schwerpunkt	Beispiel
1.	Partizip der Gegenwart	What a *boring* story!
2.	Partizip der Vergangenheit	We are *bored* to death.

TEST 1: Glückssache: *luck, be lucky* oder *be happy*?

1. Heidi was _______ Bernd was out. But she wasn't _______.
2. Tom is _______. He has got a wife and a car, and they both work.
3. Best wishes for a _______ and successful[1] first marriage.
4. Success[2] is just a matter of _______. Ask a failure[3].

1 erfolgreich 2 Erfolg 3 Versager

Meanwhile Bernd and Miss Mable had one or two whiskies *poured* by the *practised* hand of Swindler himself. He seemed to be excited about something but said nothing. Carrying the drinks over to the table Swindler began to *twitch* and *giggle*. Miss Mable was not amused.

eingießen; geübt

zucken; kichern

M: Having visited the zoo twice already, this year, I *hardly* need any demonstrations of your *relationship* to the animal world, Mr Swindler.

S: Well, it's *the knowledge of this world* we live in that is *bearing* heavily *on* my shoulders. Miss Mable, I ...

M: I'm sure that Bernd, or "Room Six" as you call him is too *tired* and also too *worried* to listen to your interesting *experience* of the world. Perhaps tomorrow. Good night.

kaum; Verwandtschaft
Lebenserfahrung
lasten ... auf
müde; besorgt
Erfahrung

TEST 2: Vier Verben – acht Partizipien

Leiten Sie von den Verben in Klammern die passenden Partizipien ab.

1. Swindler thought he had ____________ news. But Mable was not ____________. (*interest*)

2. Swindler thought he was ____________. But Miss Mable was not ____________. (*amuse*)

3. Bernd is too ____________ to listen to Swindler's ____________ experience of the world. (*tire*)

4. Blake was ____________ when he found Heidi half-naked. "What an ____________ girl!" he thought. (*excite*)

Present Participles in action

A couple *walking* in the park noticed a young man and woman *sitting* on a bench, *kissing* passionately[1]. "Why don't *you* do that?" said the wife. – "But darling," replied her husband, "I don't even know that woman!"

1 leidenschaftlich

25 Let's go back to the *safe-house.* Minutes after Blake and Heidi had made their *escape* a car *pulled up* outside the house. The Captain ran as quickly as he could and pushed the door which was *ajar.* Entering the room the Captain *smelt* alcohol. He looked down at Sam, his face *darkening.* "Sam ... Sam ... What the hell is going on? Where's Blake?" There was no *reply.* The Captain *bent* over him coming a little closer. "He's bloody well *drunk.* He's risked the whole operation. The *traitor.*" The Captain ran into the bedroom. It was empty. "Well, I suppose the diamonds have gone with them." He rushed back. There was the suitcase. He *swung* it *open.* "Damn me, they're all there. Right. Time to *abandon ship.* And you, Sam, will be no *loss* at all to me."
The Captain threw Sam over his shoulder and *heaved* him out to the car. The Captain climbed in and drove off.

Versteck
Flucht; vorfahren
angelehnt
riechen
verfinstern
Antwort
sich beugen über
betrunken
Verräter
aufstoßen
das sinkende Schiff; verlassen
hieven

TEST 3: Partizipien verkürzen Nebensätze

Beispiel: *When he saw* Sam, Dick was confused.
Seeing Sam, Dick was confused.

1. *While Swindler was serving* the drinks he began to giggle.
2. *When the Captain entered* the room he smelt alcohol.
3. He looked down at Sam *and his face darkened.*
4. An oyster is a fish *which is built* like a nut.
5. The serious music lover is the type who, *when he hears* a soprano in the bathroom, puts his ear to the keyhole.

TEST 4: Sagen Sie es mit ähnlichen Worten

There was no *answer.*	There was no r_ _ _ _ _ _ _ _
Time to *leave the ship.*	Time to a_ _ _ _ _ _ _ _ _ _ _ _
He *hurried* back.	He r_ _ _ _ _ _ _ back.
I *guess* they have disappeared.	I s_ _ _ _ _ _ _ they have gone.

Half an hour later the Captain was driving up a wet *muddy* road to a *disused quarry.* Dick (**D**) was waiting for him.	*matschig; stillgelegter Steinbruch*
D: You managed it then. Is she dead?	
The Captain *threw* Sam on the ground. Seeing Sam, Dick was confused.	*werfen*
D: What's this then? I thought you said you were bringing some *foreign* girl.	*ausländisch*
C: There's been a change of plan. It makes no *difference* to you, does it?	*Unterschied*
D: Well, ehm, no. Hey, he's not dead.	
C: No, not yet. *Does it matter*? Look, I'll double your money.	*etwas ausmachen*
D: Dead or alive, they always sink deep in the *concrete.* (He laughs *sickly*)	*Beton* *krank*
C: Okay. You *get that sorted out.* I'm *going into hiding.* Things have got too hot.	*regeln; untertauchen*
And the Captain *sets off* to Brighton.	*sich aufmachen*

TEST 5: Was versteckt sich hinter 's?

1. *Heidi's* had a fit of conscience.	Heidi *has had...*
2. Oh, *that's* good of you.	________
3. *Let's* go back to the safe-house.	________
4. *It's* all happened so quickly.	________
5. *Sam's* bloody well drunk.	________
6. *He's* risked the whole operation.	________
7. *There's* been a change of plan.	________

TEST 6: Ergänzen Sie die Indirekte Rede

1. Somebody's after me.	Heidi told Swindler ...
2. Where's the foreign girl?	Dick asked ...
3. There's been a change of plan.	He told Dick ...
4. Sam's risked the whole plan.	The Captain feared ...

26 catching up with the captain

Miss Mable and her *sidekick* Bernd arrived in Dover at nine in the morning. A *quarter* of an hour later they were standing in front of the door at number fourteen. Miss Mable looked as if she were ready to *break into a run.*

M: Aha. As I thought. The door is half open. So much for nobody being at home. Let's go in.
B: It's empty now. If only we had got in yesterday evening.
M: Indeed. Ah, here's a bedroom. Look, somebody, *obviously* Heidi, had been tied up here. Look at the rope. It has been tied, cut and retied. Hmm. Very strange. Our *bogus inspector* was here, too.
B: Yes, there's his *ashtray* and the sweet-smelling tobacco.
M: Alcohol was being *enjoyed*, I *dare* say. And lots of it. Yesterday I could smell a candle that had just been *snuffed out*. And here it is.
B: I think it's time we *paid a visit* to Brighton. Maybe they went there.

Gehilfe
Viertel (-stunde)
losrennen
offensichtlich
falscher Inspektor
Aschenbecher
genießen; wagen
ausdrücken
Besuch abstatten

Auf einen BLICK

Wiederholung einiger Schwerpunkte	
1. Mixed Grammar Revision	Passiv, If-Sätze
2. Diverse Sprachfallen	*remind, remember* etc.

TEST 1: Wie lautet die Passivform?

1. They *blocked* the road.	The road __________.
2. They *forced* the car to stop.	The car __________ to stop.
3. They had tied Heidi up.	Heidi __________ up.
4. They *had cut* the rope.	The rope __________.
5. They *had snuffed out* the candle.	The candle __________.
6. They *were enjoying* alcohol.	Alcohol __________.

Outside on the street Miss Mable was *muttering* to herself. — *murmeln*

M: Of course, we must go to Brighton, but this time I'd rather take the police with me. We're arriving at a critical point. Let's go to the *nearest* telephone box and phone that friendly sergeant. He knows the *background* to all this.
B: Miss Mable. We don't need to *search for* a phone-box. I have *borrowed* Jenny's mobile to help in emergencies.
M: That young lady is *turning out to be* most *useful* and *reliable.* You've been seeing her now and again, haven't you? *Suppose* Heidi suddenly *turns up.* I'd rather not *be in your shoes.*
B: Oh, things will sort themselves out.

nächstgelegen; Hintergrund; suchen nach; sich leihen; Notfall; sich erweisen als; nützlich; zuverlässig; angenommen; auftauchen; in jemandes Haut stecken

But Bernd *felt his heart sink.* Meanwhile Miss Mable was speaking to the sergeant. — *das Herz fiel ihm in die Hose*

M: Good morning, sergeant. You'll remember me. Miss Mable. I think it's time I asked you for your help.

TEST 2: Was ist das Gegenteil der kursiven Worte?

1. A car began to *pull out* down the road.	______________
2. Jenny is turning out to be *reliable.*	______________
3. The mobile phone is most *useful.*	______________
4. They *lighted* a candle.	______________

TEST 3: Ergänzen Sie die Verbformen

1. Customer, at a repair shop: Please change the oil.
Mechanic: If I were you, I (*keep*) the oil and change the car.

2. My wife says she (*leave*) me if I don't throw out my computer. I will miss her.

26 The sergeant was *as good as his word.* The police car arrived ten minutes later, of course *with lights flashing and sirens howling.* On the way Miss Mable explained her *fears* to the sergeant.

zu seinem Wort stehen; mit Blaulicht und Sirene
Befürchtung

M: You see, sergeant, it's high time we *caught up with* these criminals. I do hope the girl is still *safe and sound. All the clues indicate* that this "inspector" Reed is ready to *take* some sort of *action.*

einholen
wohlauf sein; alles weist darauf hin
zur Tat schreiten

S: What makes you so sure about all this?

M: May I *remind* you of a few *items* I *mentioned* before. The suitcase was the first *clue.* It led us to Dover. Then there was the Dutch tobacco *smell* in the suitcase and in the house in Dover. But most important, somebody was in the house yesterday when we *called round.* So they knew we *were onto them.* Now we know that Heidi had been there. And I think I've identified their new safe house in Brighton. I don't know if we'll *be in time.*

erinnern; Punkt; erwähnen; Hinweis; Geruch
vorbeischauen; an jemandem dran sein
rechtzeitig kommen

catching up with the captain

TEST 4: Intelligentes Raten

Nummerieren Sie die Reihenfolge der Schritte.
Übersetzen Sie das Kursivgedruckte.

	Release the *handbrake.*	________
	Press the *accelerator*, drive away.	________
1	Put the key into the *ignition.*	________
	Put the car into first *gear.*	________
	Release the clutch very slowly.	________
	Push in the clutch.	________
	Turn it and start the *engine.*	________

The police car *pulled up* outside 6, The Mews, Brighton.	*vorfahren*
The house was dark. A policeman got out, walked up to the door and pressed the doorbell. *Silence.* A car began to *pull out* down the road. Miss Mable shouted loudly.	*Stille; wegfahren*

M: Sergeant, that's him. Stop that car!
S: Are you sure? How do you know?
M: Just do it!

The sergeant dropped the car into *first gear* and pressed	*erster Gang*
the *accelerator* hard so that the car sprang into the	*Gaspedal*
middle of the road. He *hit the brake* aggressively caus-	*auf die Bremse*
ing the car to *skid* around. The road was blocked. The	*treten; schleudern*
approaching car was *forced* to stop.	*näher kommen*
	zwingen

S: I wish you'd tell me why you're so sure it's him.
M: Well, it's simple really. You see he looks just like I *imagined* him. The perfect gentleman, dressed in tweeds. And he's smoking a pipe. It's time we met *at last*.

sich vorstellen · *endlich*

TEST 5: Streichen Sie den falschen Ausdruck

1. I have *borrowed / have lent* Jenny's mobile to help in emergencies.
2. Jenny *borrowed / lent* me her mobile to help in emergencies.
3. Let's go to the *next / nearest* telephone box.
4. The phone's out of order. Let's try the *next / nearest* phone-box.
5. We *needn't / mustn't search for* a phone-box. I've got a mobile.
6. May I *remember / remind* you of a few items I mentioned before.
7. You'll *remember / remind* me, sergeant, won't you?

Time for a smile

Thieves escaped with over 600,000 euros in a robbery. The police are trying to find a motive for the crime.

27 showdown at the mews

The sergeant ran over to the car. The pipe-smoking gentleman was already *winding down* his window. "You nearly ran into me. What's it all about, officer?" The sergeant stepped forward. Miss Mable *joined* him at the car. The policeman stood up to his *full height*. "We've been looking for you for some time. We have *reason to believe* that you were involved in the *abduction* of a young German tourist a week ago." The Captain, for it was indeed him, looked *amazed*.	*herunterkurbeln*; *sich anschließen*; *volle Größe*; *Grund zur Annahme*; *Entführung*; *verblüfft*
C: I think you've mixed me up with somebody. I've just had a holiday in the Lake District. I'm trying to *get over the flu*, you know.	*eine Grippe auskurieren*
At this moment Miss Mable interrupted.	
M: Come along, my good man. The German girl has *spilled the beans on* you. Or we wouldn't have found this house, would we?	*alles auspacken*
Of course Miss Mable was bluffing. If Heidi were already dead, the Captain would know that. If she were still *alive* his reactions would show it, too. It all happened *in a flash*.	*am Leben*; *blitzschnell*

Auf einen BLICK

Schwerpunkt	Beispiel
1. Der Platz der Adverbien	You *nearly* ran into me.
2. Übersetzung von *lassen*	leave a message

TEST 1: Verbinden Sie die Sätze durch *ing*-Formen

1. The sergeant sprang backwards. He looked at the gun.
2. She stuck her umbrella through the window. She opened it out like an airbag.
3. Heidi phoned yesterday. She wanted to know where the suitcase was.

The Captain *whipped* a pistol from the side pocket of his car and fired a *shot* which *hit* his *mirror.* The sergeant sprang backwards, looking at the gun which was *pointed* directly *at* his heart.	*zücken* *Schuss; treffen* *Spiegel* *richten auf*
S: You might *as well give up*. You can't *get away* with this.	*ruhig aufgeben* *davonkommen*
C: (*Hissing* between his teeth) Well, I'm damn well going to try.	*zischen*
At that moment there was a noise as Bernd sprinted towards the *passenger door* of the car. Of course, there was no chance to get the door open, but Bernd had *gained* them a *split second.* The Captain was *off his guard* for less than one or two seconds, just long enough for the *prying* pensioner to stick her *umbrella* through the window opening it out like an airbag. The Captain couldn't see anything for a few seconds. These few seconds *came across as an eternity,* but it was long enough for the sergeant to pull open the door and throw himself across the Captain. It was over *in a flash.* The sergeant phoned for a *Black Maria.* An inspection of the house gave no *further clues.* There was no Heidi. And *in any case* why had the Captain kidnapped her at all?	*Beifahrertür* *gewinnen; Sekundenbruchteil; unachtsam; neugierig; Regenschirm* *wie eine Ewigkeit erscheinen* *blitzschnell; Grüne Minna; weitere Hinweise; auf alle Fälle*

TEST 2: Wohin mit den Adverbien?

Setzen Sie die Adverbien in Klammern an den richtigen Platz.

1. You ran into me.	(*nearly*)
2. He was winding down his window.	(*already*)
3. I've had a holiday in the Lake District.	(*just*)
4. I got through to Jenny at the hospital.	(*just*)
5. Oh, it's you, Miss Mable.	(*only*)
6. The flying foreigner was here.	(*yesterday*)

27 *showdown at the mews*

Miss Mable felt there were still a lot of *question marks* in the whole story. The sergeant came into the house.	*Fragezeichen*
S: Miss Mable. I think we've *come across* the motive for this crime.	*stoßen auf*
M: Good, there are certainly some *gaps* we have to fill in.	*Lücken*
S: Mr Reed had a suitcase half full of diamonds in his car. I'd *put* it *at* half a million pounds. That's certainly *worth* a kidnapping.	*schätzen auf*; *lohnen*
M: Good, but that doesn't *help us further* with the girl, Heidi.	*weiterhelfen*
At this point Bernd, who had been on Jenny's mobile, walked through the door.	
S: Miss Mable. I just *got through to* Jenny at the hospital. *Apparently* Heidi phoned her yesterday wanting to know where our suitcase was.	*telefonisch erreichen; anscheinend*
M: Which is, of course, in our hotel. Can you phone Swindler *straight away*. I'll talk to him.	*umgehend*
S: Heidi told Jenny to let me know that she's okay and not to worry.	
M: Hmm! (She *calls* Holiday Out *immediately*)	*anrufen; sofort*

TEST 3: Wie übersetzt man *lassen*?

1. The sergeant _______ _____ a prison car. (*kommen lassen*)
2. Heidi _____ him _____ that she was okay. (*wissen lassen*)
3. She ________ a message for room six. (*hinterlassen*).
4. Swindler ______ Heidi ______ her bill before he ____ her ____ her passport. (*hinterlassen, überlassen*).
5. On holiday, people drive thousands of miles just to _________ their picture _________ in front of their cars. (*machen lassen*)

S:	Hello, Holiday Out, the best real English holiday that man, woman or dog could ever *dream of*. How can I *make your day*?	*träumen* *glücklich machen*
M:	Mr Swindler, will you please put aside your *sales twaddle*!	*Verkaufsgeschwätz*
S:	Oh, it's only you, Miss Mable. I was hoping for some new blood.	
M:	Your vampire *needs* don't interest me at present. I would like to know if anything unusual has happened in the last twenty-four hours.	*Bedürfnis*
S:	Well, some *unexpected bills* were paid, and some people shot in and out like a boomerang.	*unerwartete Rechnungen*
M:	Mr Swindler. You're *waffling*. Can you be more precise? I'm *referring to* the girl, Heidi.	*faseln* *meinen*
S:	Ho ho! You mean Miss "here for breakfast, gone by lunch."	
M:	Mr Swindler. Please.	
S:	Yes, yes. The *flying foreigner* was here yesterday *alive and kicking*. She wanted her passport but I made her pay her bill first. She left a message for room six.	*fliegender Ausländer; quicklebendig*
M:	Thank you, Mr Swindler. It's all becoming clear at last	

TEST 4: Wo ist der Platz des Adverbs?

1. A wise husband laughs at his wife's old clothes. (*never*)
2. A husband's last words are, "Okay, buy it." (*always*)
3. I surprised my wife with a mink coat. She'd seen me in one. (*never*)
4. I arrive late at the office, but I make up for it by leaving early. (*always*)
5. Some errors will go unnoticed until the book is in print. (*always*)
6. God would have given us the bicycle, if he had wanted us to walk. (*never*)

28 all's well that ends well

Well, that's the end of the story. Or to *put it in a nutshell* "that's all we're going to tell you of Bernd and Heidi's trip to England." Maybe some of you who *are into* this *trivial* type of literature would like to have the *ends tidied up* and read more about our heroes. Why not indeed?

kurz gesagt
mögen
banal
klarer Abschluss

So, what's first? Perhaps that poor *underling*, Sam. Even though he was probably a swine and a killer, still it's not very *comfortable* to be *buried* alive in liquid concrete even if it comes from a high quality *manufacturer.* Don't panic! It didn't happen. Dick didn't *intend* to do it. He's okay with burying the already dead. However, he doesn't work with living *flesh.* So Sam got away with it and simply *disappeared.*

Handlanger
angenehm; begraben; Hersteller
beabsichtigen
Fleisch
verschwinden

Then there was Blake and Heidi. A rather *instantaneous* friendship. Blake managed to sell the diamonds and got about £150,000. It's better than a *kick in the backside.* At present they are on the Island of Barbados, and, would you believe, Heidi is studying *economics.*

plötzlich
Tritt in den Hintern
Wirtschaftswissenschaften

That brings us to the other couple. Bernd felt strange but also strangely *relieved.* He left Holiday Out and took a *flat share* in Hastings. He sees Jenny regularly. They are "going out", as it were. Bernd is also doing a *part-time course* in computers and teaches ten hours a week in a local college. Bernd and Jenny ... but this is a different story.

erleichtert
Wohngemeinschaft
Halbtagskurs

Miss Mable will be Miss Mable. As a *permanent guest* of Holiday Out she'll certainly run into more *hair-raising* adventures. Read on!

Dauergast
haarsträubend

And last but not least, Swindler. Well, he was and remains a tricky and a crooked fellow. What can we say about him? Well, he had a visit from the *health and*

Gesundheitsamt

hygiene authorities. There had been talk of rats, but strangely enough none were found.
By coincidence Swindler introduced a new "special" on his menu. He called it his very *tender* "Argentinian *rabbit stew.*" As Swindler always says "waste not, want not."

Hope you enjoyed it! Watch out for further adventures of old Mable at Swindler's place.

zufällig
zart
Kaninchenragout

KEY : Der Schlüssel zu den Tests

CHAPTER 1

TEST 1: Beherrschen Sie die Vorvergangenheit

1. **B.** Mr Swindler *came* into some money *after* his aunt *had passed* away.
2. **A.** Mr Swindler, *who had come* into some money, *bought* the mansion.
   B. *After* Mr Swindler *had come* into some money he *bought* the mansion.
3. His aunt, *who had been* a teacher for 30 years *passed* away on the 30th of August.

TEST 2: Mit anderen Worten

1. Ron *got* some money.	Ron *came into* some money.
2. His aunt *died* quietly.	His aunt quietly *passed away.*
3. He *changed* the rooms to apartments	He *converted* them to apartments.

TEST 3: Richtig (R) oder falsch (F)

	R	F
1. The mansion had at least twelve bedrooms.	✔	
2. The mansion was built in the nineteenth century.		✔
3. Mr Swindler got it from his aunt.		✔
4. The kitchens are in the cellar.	✔	

TEST 4: Übersetzen Sie

A man walks into a hotel and asks, "Do you take children?"
The receptionist replies, "No, only cash and traveller's cheques."

CHAPTER 2

TEST 1: Meistern Sie den Imperativ

1. *"Don't worry,"* a patient told his psychiatrist. "I'll pay every penny I owe, or my name isn't Alexander the Great!"
2. Patient: Shall I start at the beginning?
   Doctor: *Do* that, please.
   Patient: Well, in the beginning I created Heaven and Earth.
3. Tom: *Don't you pull* faces at my parrot! He's very sensitive.
   Bob: All right, but he started it!

TEST 2: Probleme mit den kleinen Wörtern?

1. Heidi and Bernd are eager *to* spend some time in England.
2. Their holidays start *on* August 1st.
3. They are preparing *for* their journey.
4. They look *at* a travel brochure.
5. They will travel *by* car.
6. They get a move *on*.

TEST 3: Englisch am Telefon – Was fehlt hier?

Guten Tag. Was kann ich für Sie tun?	Good morning. What *can* I do *for* you?
Darf ich nach dem Grund Ihres Anrufs fragen?	Could I *ask* the purpose of your *call*?
Es geht um Ihre Annonce.	It's *about* your advert.
Ich rufe an, um ein Zimmer zu reservieren.	I'm *phoning* to *book* a room.

TEST 4: Word Power – Was ist gemeint?

1. Place where you plan to arrive at	*destination*
2. There they deal with people who arrive	*reception*
3. Say that you are not happy	*complain*
4. The hotel belongs to him	*owner*

TEST 5: Idiomatisches Englisch – Erinnern Sie sich?

1. *Beeil dich!*	Get a *move* on!
2. *Du hast's immer so eilig.*	You're always *rushing*.
3. *Lass mich in Ruhe!*	*Leave* me alone!
4. *Es geht mich nichts an.*	It's not my *business*.

TEST 6: Haben Sie verstanden? Right (R) or Wrong (W)?

	R	F
1. One night at the Holiday Out hotel is €60.	✔	
2. They will have to pay in advance.		✔
3. Our couple's holiday starts on August 1st.	✔	
4. They will travel in their own car.		✔
5. Mr Swindler has a gardener and a chamber maid.		✔

CHAPTER 3

TEST 1: Kreuzen Sie die falsche Verbform an

3. Heidi, ~~are you having~~ *do* you *have* your driving licence?

Warum ist 3. falsch?
Have ist ein *statisches* Verb, wenn es *haben* = *besitzen* bedeutet. *Siehe unten* (Aber: We *are having* a party: Wir *feiern* gerade. Hier ist *have a party* eine Tätigkeit, ein *dynamisches* Verb.

✪ Globalregel ✪

1. ***Simple Forms*** für Dauerzustände und oft wiederholte Vorgänge.

Der Neckar fließt in den Rhein.	The Neckar *flows* into the Rhine.
Tom schreibt Romane.	Tom *writes* novels.

2. ***Progressive Forms*** für zeitlich begrenzte Vorgänge, die zu einem Zeitpunkt im Verlauf, d.h. nicht abgeschlossen sind.

Der Neckar fließt *heute* schnell.	The Neckar *is flowing* rapidly today.
Tom schreibt einen Brief.	Tom *is writing* a letter.

3. **Statische Verben (Zustandsverben) stehen im *Simple Tense*.**

a. Zustandsverben:
be, have, contain, belong, possess, want, need, own

b. Verben, die eine Eigenschaft bedeuten und durch *be* ersetzt werden könnten:
taste, smell, look, feel, seem, cost
c. Verben der Sinneswahrnehmung: *see, hear, notice, mind*
d. Verben des Wissens, Glaubens, Meinens:
believe, expect (= think), know, mean, think, understand, want

TEST 2: Sagen Sie es mit anderen Worten

1. *What* can I *do for* you?	*How* can I *help* you?
2. The next train *leaves* at 8:15.	The next train *departs* at 8:15.
3. What *shall we* do?	What *are we going* to do?
4. We'd like to *rent* a car.	We'd like to *hire* a car.

TEST 3: Wodurch unterscheiden sich Satz A und Satz B?

A: Oh, *do be* quiet.	B: Oh, *be* quiet.
A: *Do be* careful.	B: *Be* careful.

Mit *do / does* wird eine Aussage betont.

TEST 4: Erinnern Sie sich an das Gegenteil?

1. It's a *permanent* licence.	It's a *temporary* licence.
2. They *spent* thirty euros.	They *saved* thirty euros.
3. It's the *same* in Britain.	It's *different* in Britain.
4. It's *easy*.	It's a bit *difficult*.
5. It's the *most expensive* one.	It's the *cheapest* one.

TEST 5: Und welche Verbformen sind hier falsch?

2. What *do* you *want*?

Want ist ein statisches Verb, siehe oben.

CHAPTER 4

TEST 1: Bilden Sie Sätze (Vorsicht mit den Verbformen)

1. Tom and Tina *are* now *sitting* in a sports car.
2. Tina *is driving* smoothly along the roads.
3. Suddenly Tina *sees* a cow on the road.
4. Tina *hits* the brakes.
5. She *misses* the cow.
6. She *crashes* into a tree.

✪ Wenn zu einem Zeitpunkt (**3.** *Suddenly* ...) eine Aktivität (**1.** sit und **2.** drive) schon und noch im Gang ist, steht die Verlaufsform. Ausdrücke wie *at the moment, still, now* können ein Signal für die Verlaufsform sein.
Aufeinander folgende Handlungen (Handlungskette **3**, **4**, **5**, **6**) stehen in der einfachen Form.
Das dramatische Präsens wird in Erzählungen oft statt der Vergangenheit gewählt.

TASK 2: Fragewörter

1. *Why* are you driving so fast?
2. *Whose* fault is it?
3. *What's* the number of the emergency services?

TEST 3: Welche Verbform wählen Sie?

1. They *are driving* on narrow country roads when suddenly an animal *jumps* in front of them.
2. Heidi *looks* after Bernd while the constable *writes* the report.
3. Bernd *is* still *breathing* when the ambulance *arrives.*

TEST 4: Korrigieren Sie die Fehler

P: Do you want a phone? (*want* ist ein statisches Verb)
H: No, *I still have* my mobile.
(*have* im Sinne von besitzen ist statisch!, d.h. keine Verlaufsform)
Oh, good, it'*s ringing* now. (Die Aktivität ist zum Zeitpunkt des Sprechens schon und noch im Verlauf)
P: OK. I still *need* five minutes to write this report.
(*need* ist ein statisches Verb!)
Zu statischen und dynamischen Verben siehe *Key* zu *chapter* 3, S. 122, 123

TEST 5: Wissen Sie, was das "it" ist?

It	shows how much petrol you have left.	*petrol gauge*
It	has a glove compartment.	*dashboard*
It	is a meter that shows your speed.	*speedometer*
It	is a meter that shows your mileage.	*milometer*
It	is a pedal. You press it to change gear.	*clutch (Kupplung)*

TEST 6: Was ist das Gegenteil?

a *final report*	a *preliminary* report
the *bottom left* hand corner	the *top right* hand corner
it takes *more* than an hour	it takes *less* than an hour
a *wide* country road	a *narrow* country road

TEST 7: Das Auto – Erraten Sie das Kursivgedruckte

1.	Could you *fill her up*, please?	*volltanken*
2.	Please change the *bulb* in the *headlight.*	*Birne, Scheinwerfer*
3.	I've got a *puncture.* Could you fit the *spare*, please?	*Platten, Ersatzreifen*
4.	Could you *tow* us to the nearest service garage?	*abschleppen*
5.	It won't start. Could you *give it a push*, please?	*anschieben*

TEST 8: Für den Fall der Fälle

1. Calm down.
2. Put up warning triangle and a flashing light.
3. Look after the injured persons.
4. Call **999.** Ask for an ambulance, if necessary.
5. Wait for the ambulance and the police.
6. Report the accident to the police.
7. Fill in the accident report.

CHAPTER 5

TEST 1: Modale Horrormistakes

		Falsch	Richtig
1.	Ich kann Englisch.	*I can English.*	I can *speak* English.
2.	Ich kann es.	*I can it.*	I can *do* it.
3.	Du musst es nicht.	*You must not do it.*	You *needn't do* it.
4.	Er muss es können.	*He must can it.*	He must *be able* to *do* it.

Merke:
zu 1, 2, 3: *Modals* stehen selten allein. Sie werden durch ein Verb ergänzt, das im Deutschen oft wegfällt
zu 4: Würden zwei *modals* aufeinander treffen, nimmt man für das zweite eine Ersatzform.

TEST 2: *Simple Past* oder *Past Progressive*?

1. We *were driving* along a road when a deer *ran* into the car.
2. Neither of us *was drinking* while we *were driving.*
3. We *were arguing* at the time the accident *happened.*

Globalregel

Progressive für zeitlich begrenzte Vorgänge(**1**, **3**), die zu einem Zeitpunkt (hier in der Vergangeheit) im Verlauf, d.h. nicht abgeschlossen sind.
Progressive auch für zwei parallele, gleichzeitig verlaufende dynamische Situationen. Sie sind oft durch ***while*** verbunden (**2**).

TEST 3: Lassen Sie sich nicht einschüchtern

Ich weigere mich auszusagen.	I *refuse* to *give* evidence.
Hier steht Aussage gegen Aussage.	It's your word *against* ours.
Ich möchte einen Anwalt sprechen.	I'd like to *speak* to a *lawyer.*
Kann ich eine Kopie des Protokolls haben?	Can I have a *copy* of the official *report*?

TEST 4: Wohin mit dem Arztvokabular?

1.	Are you privately *insured*?	Sind Sie privat *versichert*?
2.	Please get undressed to the *waist.*	Machen Sie den *Oberkörper* frei.
3.	Hold your *breath*.	Halten Sie den *Atem* an.
4.	Have you been *vaccinated* against tetanus?	Sind Sie gegen Wundstarrkrampf *geimpft*?
5.	We need to take an *X-ray.*	Wir müssen eine *Röntgenaufnahme* machen.
6.	I need a blood *sample*.	Ich brauche eine *Blutprobe*.
7.	I'll give you a *prescription.*	Ich gebe Ihnen ein *Rezept*.
8.	Take these pills three *times* a day.	Nehmen Sie diese Tabletten *dreimal täglich.*

CHAPTER 6

TEST 1: Vokabelprobleme aus vorangehenden Kapiteln

near, next oder *nearest?*

Wer ist der Nächste?	Who's *next*?
Wo ist das nächste Hotel?	Where is the *nearest* hotel?
Die Bar ist nahe der Rezeption.	The bar is *near to* the reception.

ago, before oder *in front of?*

Es geschah vor drei Tagen.	It happened *three days ago.*
Sie kam vor Mitternacht an.	She arrived *before* midnight.
Sie wartete vor dem Hotel.	She waited *in front of* the hotel.

TEST 2: Warum *Simple Present* Tense?

Constable Smith *presses* the doorbell, *climbs* into his car and *disappears.* The door *opens* and a figure *appears* in the *doorframe.*

1. ***Simple Present*** Tense, weil es sich um eine Kette abgeschlossener Situationen handelt und
2. ***Simple Present*** Tense, weil es sich um das dramatische Präsens handelt.

TEST 3: Noch mehr Wortschatzprobleme?

luck, lucky oder *happy, happiness?*

1. Sie haben Glück gehabt.	You were *lucky.*
2. Sie sehen nicht glücklich aus.	You don't look *happy* today.
3. Ihre Augen glänzten vor Glück.	Her eyes shone with *happiness.*

at least oder *at last?*

Tina must be *at least* 70. She is slow but *at least* reliable.
At last Tom arrived. I had been waiting for *at least* an hour.

TEST 4: Und warum *Simple Present* Tense hier?

People often *don't arrive* after they've booked. You can't *rely* on anybody. They *come* and they *go*. Then nothing *works* any more.

3. Swindler spricht von Situationen, die sich immer wieder ereignen.

TEST 5: Worte an der Rezeption

Für mich ist ein Zimmer reserviert worden.	There is a room *reserved* for me here.
Wir sind leider ausgebucht.	I'm afraid, we're fully *booked.*
Wir haben kein Zimmer frei.	We don't have any *vacancies.*
Aber Sie haben die Buchung per Fax bestätigt.	But you *confirmed* the booking by fax.
Wie lange bleiben Sie?	How long will you be *staying*?
Möchten Sie Vollpension oder nur Frühstück?	Do you want *full* board or only breakfast?
Gibt es eine Ermäßigung für Geschäftsleute?	Is there a *reduction* for business-people?
Füllen Sie bitte das Anmeldungsformular aus.	Please fill in the registration *form.*
Angenehmen Aufenthalt.	Enjoy your *stay.*

CHAPTER 7

TEST 1: Die Zeiten begleiten uns weiter

1. She *picked up* the wrong suitcase when she *was waiting* at the hospital.
2. She *switched* the TV on and *lay down* on the bed.
3. Half past ten at the hospital. Bernd *was feeling* good.
4. "I *thought* you *wanted* to sign out this morning," said the nurse.

Merke:

Satz 1, 3: Situation 1 (*She picked up. / Half past ten*) markiert eine abgeschlossene Handlung bzw. einen Zeitpunkt in der Vergangenheit. Deshalb steht einfache Vergangenheit.
Situation 2 (*was waiting, was feeling*) war zu dem Zeitpunkt schon und noch im Verlauf. Deshalb Verlaufsform in der Vergangenheit.
Satz 2: Aufeinander folgende Situationen stehen in der einfachen Vergangenheit (*Simple Past*).
Satz 4: Zeitenfolge in der indirekten Rede: I *thought,* deshalb *you wanted.*

TEST 2: Kurzformen für Eigentümer

1. The suitcase doesn't belong to *us*. It's not *ours*.
2. And it isn't *my* suitcase. It isn't *mine*.
3. Perhaps it's *Mr Swindler's* suitcase. Perhaps it's *his*.
4. They may be *Mrs Swindler's* jewels. They might be *hers*.
5. It's not *Bernd and Heidi's* suitcase. Anyway, it's not *theirs*.
6. And, dear reader, they aren't *your* diamonds either. They aren't *yours* either.

✪ **Merke:** *mine, yours, his, hers, ours, yours, theirs* sind die substantivischen Possessivpronomen.

TEST 3: Noch mehr Zeitprobleme

1. After Bernd *had left* Jenny, he *thought* about life in general.

2. After two minutes Bernd *gave* up. Nobody *had lifted* the phone.

Situation 1 (Bernd *gave up*, he *thought*) passierte in der Vergangenheit.
Situation 2 (*had left, had lifted*) passierte in der Vorvergangenheit.

3. If you *give me* your number I'*ll pay* you back.

Bedingungssatz Typ I: *Present Tense* im if Satz,
Will-Future im Hauptsatz.

4. If you *gave* me your number I *would invite* you to dinner, too.

Bedingungssatz Typ II: *Past Tense* im if Satz,
Konditional im Hauptsatz.

TEST 4: leihen – *borrow* oder *lend*?

1. A consultant is someone who *borrows* your watch to tell you what time it is and then walks away with it.
2. A banker is a fellow who *lends* you his umbrella when the sun is shining and wants it back when it begins to rain.
3. Always *borrow* money from a pessimist. He doesn't expect to get it back.

✪ **Merke:** *borrow* sich etwas von jemandem (aus-)leihen
lend jemandem etwas leihen

TEST 5: Mit der Vermittlung sprechen

Welche Nummer *versuchen* Sie zu erreichen?	What number *are* you *trying* to get / reach?
Verbinden Sie mich bitte mit Holiday Out.	Please *connect* me with Holiday Out.
Ich *verbinde* Sie.	I'*m putting* you through.
Bleiben Sie bitte am Apparat!	*Hold* the line, please.
Tut mir Leid, ich kann ihn nicht *erreichen.*	Sorry, I can't *get* his number.
Die Rufnummer hat sich *geändert.*	The number has been *changed.*
Die neue Nummer ist ...	The new number is ...
Einen Augenblick. Sie *werden verbunden.*	One moment. It's *ringing* for you.

CHAPTER 8

TEST 1: Bilden Sie das Passiv

1. An egg is something that *is never beaten* when it is bad.
2. High heels *were invented by a woman* who didn't like *to be kissed* on her forehead.
3. A pessimist is a man *who has been forced* to live with an optimist.

TEST 2: *eigen* = *own* – eine Falle für Deutsche

1. Ich sah es mit *eigenen* Augen.	I saw it with *my own* eyes.
2. Ich habe ein *eigenes* Zimmer.	I've got a room *of my own.*
3. *Sein eigener* Sohn war der Dieb.	*His own* son was the thief.
4. Er tat es auf *eigene Faust.*	He did it *on his own.*

Merke: *own* (Adjektiv) kommt in drei Strukturen vor:

1. nach Possessivpronomen	He has got *his own* car.
2. nach of-Genitiv mit Possessivpronomen	He has got a car *of his own.*
3. nach 's-Genitiv	It is Tom*'s own* car.

ein eigenes / das eigene Haus.
Falsch: ~~an / the own house~~ **Richtig:** one's / his / our own house

TEST 3: bringen – *bring* oder *take*?

zum Sprecher *hin*-bringen	←	bring
vom Sprecher *weg*-bringen	→	take

1. "Waiter! Waiter! You've *brought* me a lobster with just one claw!" ... *take* this one away and *bring* me the winner."
2. "When I was seven years old my father *took* me to the zoo." "Were you accepted?"
3. Soldier: And what happens if the parachute fails to open? Sergeant: *Bring* it back and you'll get another.
4. But Heidi was *taken* to your hotel yesterday in the night. Yes, she was *brought* here in splendour.

TEST 4: Mr Swindler's passive complaint

1. Bills *haven't been paid.*
2. Doors *have been left open.*
3. The room *has been left* in a mess.
4. Nothing *has been arranged* with the hotel.
5. The missing person *hasn't been reported* to the police.

CHAPTER 9

TEST 1: Vergangenheit oder Vorvergangenheit?

1. In the evening Bernd *went* back to the hotel. In the afternoon he *had dropped* in at the police-station.
2. His room *had* not *been cleaned* and he *was* not really surprised.
3. He *had* hardly *had* anything to eat in two days with all this stress.

TEST 2: Was bedeutet das einfache *Will-Future*?

1.	I'*ll take* the lamb.	D
2.	And you *will like* it.	A, B
3.	Swindler is so mean he *will* not *employ* people to help him.	C
4.	At my age *you will* learn to take it easy.	A

TEST 3: Das *Will-Future* der Verlaufsform, A, B oder C?

1.	Mr Swindler *will be arriving* in a minute. He always does.	B
2.	And, what *will* sir *be drinking* with it?	C
3.	Hello, I know what *I'll be eating* this evening.	A
4.	I'm not sure what *I'll be getting* now.	A

TEST 4: Der große Zukunftstest für Anti-Muffel

1. Bernd:	What *am I going to do* now?	B. Vorhaben
2. Bernd:	*I'll try* the house red.	B. spontaner Entschluss
3. Swindler:	*I won't* be a minute.	A. Versprechen
4. Mable:	You're too impatient. You'*re going to get* problems with your *blood pressure.*	B. Schlussfolgerung
5.	Our son *is going to be* an auctioneer. This is the third valuable vase he has brought under the hammer.	A. Schlussfolgerung
6.	As soon as the German tourist *gets* to Paradise, he *will ask* for picture postcards.	A. typische Gewohnheit

TEST 5: Fleisch bei Swindler

1. The meet of an ox is	*beef*
2. The meat of a pig is	*pork*
3. The meat of a baby cow is	*veal*
4. The meat of a deer is	*venison*
5. Mussels and lobster are	*seafood*

TEST 6: Ergänzen Sie das Gespräch mit dem Kellner

1. *Haben Sie gewählt?*	May I *take* your orders?
2. *Was nehmen Sie als Vorspeise?*	What will you *have* for *starters*?
3. *Ich kann die Ente empfehlen.*	I can *recommend* the duck.
4. *Wie ist das Lamm zubereitet?*	How is the lamb *done*?
5. *Schreiben Sie alles auf eine Rechnung.*	Could you *put* it all on one *bill*?

CHAPTER 10

TEST 1: Erkennen Sie ein *Present Perfect*?

	Kurzform: *'s*	Langform: *is* oder *has*?
1.	There's no sign of Heidi.	There *is* no sign of Heidi.
2.	But it's all gone wrong.	But it *has* all gone wrong.
3.	Heidi's disappeared.	Heidi *has* disappeared.
4.	Heidi's a bit impulsive.	Heidi *is* a bit impulsive.
5.	But she's never done anything like that before.	But she *has* never done anything like that before.

TEST 2: *Past Tense* oder *Present Perfect*?

Mable: You *arrived* at Holiday Out yesterday.
Bernd: How *did* you know that? I haven't *mentioned* it.
Mable: *Have* you *had* any trouble with Heidi recently?
Bernd: I*'ve had* nothing but trouble.
Mable: *Have* you *checked* the local hospital?
Bernd: Yes, I *went* there yesterday.
Mable: What *have* you *done* since you *realised* she had disappeared?
Bernd: Well, *I haven't done* anything sensible so far.

Das *Present Perfect* (Präsens Perfekt) ist, wie der Name sagt, eine Zeit der Gegenwart. Man nimmt es

1. für Situationen, die bis zum Zeitpunkt des Sprechens noch nicht abgeschlossen sind (häufig mit *so far, already, never* oder *since* und *for* (seit);
2. für Situationen, die zwar abgeschlossen (perfekt), aber für die Gegenwart (Präsens) von Bedeutung sind. Wann und wo sich die Situation ereignet hat, wird nicht gesagt, weil nur das Ergebnis zählt.

TEST 3: *Mean* oder *think*?

Siehe Anmerkung zu Test 5.

1. Have you had any personal problems with Heidi recently?
   I *mean*, are you two okay together?
2. I haven't thrown the suitcase away, but I was *thinking* about it.
3. How long have you been here at Holiday Out?
   I *mean* you speak very good English.
4. You're upset. I *think* it has something to do with your girlfriend.

TEST 4: Die richtige Form – Adjektiv oder Adverb?

1. Miss Mable sat *quietly* for several minutes.
2. Mr Swindler's hotel is not a *quiet* place.
3. You're *certainly* very upset.
4. I haven't done anything *sensible* so far.
5. Nothing worth learning is learned *quickly* except parachuting.

Adjektiv und Adverb der Art und Weise

(Siehe auch Anmerkungen in key to chapter 14, Seite 140)

Wir machen keinen Unterschied zwischen Adjektiv und Adverb, die Engländer schon.

Er ist langsam.	He is **slow**.
Er isst langsam.	He eats **slowly**.

Das Adjektiv antwortet auf die Frage „Wie ist das Ding, die Person?“ Es charakterisiert ein **Substantiv**
Das Adverb der Art u. Weise charakterisiert eine **Tätigkeit**. „Wie wird etwas getan?“ Es unterscheidet sich vom Adjektiv durch das angehängte *-ly*.

TEST 5: Doppelt genäht hält besser – *mean* oder *think*?

1. Have you ever been to a zoo? I *mean as a* visitor?
2. If you *think* nothing is impossible, try getting your name off a mailing list.
3. He's a guy who can say absolutely nothing and *mean* it.

think = meinen im Sinne von glauben, halten von

Ich glaube das auch.	I think so, too.
Was meinst du dazu?	What do you think about it?

mean = meinen im Sinne von bedeuten, sagen wollen

Was bedeutet dieses Wort?	What does this word mean?
Wie meinen Sie das?	How do you mean?
Ich meine, was ich sage.	I mean what I say.

mean (to) = es ernst meinen, beabsichtigen, wollen

Ich wollte nicht unhöflich sein.	I didn't mean to be rude.
Ich meine es ernst.	I mean it.

CHAPTER 11

TEST 1: Verstehen Sie das *Present Participle*?

1. Bernd *stood listening* at the door. — Bernd stand an der Tür *und* lauschte.
2. He *came running* into the bar. — Er kam *angelaufen* ...
3. He *arrived breathing* heavily. — Er kam *heftig atmend* an.
4. Mrs Mable was still *sitting* at the bar *sipping* her wine. — Sie saß an der Bar *und* schlürfte ihren Wein.

Das *Present Participle* steht hier nach Verben der Ruhe und Bewegung. Im Deutschen werden Haupt- und Nebensatz oft durch *und* verbunden.

arrive, come, get, go, leave,
lie, remain, return, sit, stand, wait

TEST 2: Erinnern Sie sich? Wie hieß es im Text?

1. Bernd *hurried* upstairs. — Bernd *rushed* upstairs.
2. He was *searching* for his key. — He was *fumbling* for his key.
3. Did you *take away* the suitcase? — Did you *remove* the suitcase?
4. This is a *catastrophe.* — This is a *disaster.*
5. *Save money for a rainy day.* — *Waste not, want not.*

TEST 3: Sagen – *say*, *talk* oder *tell*?

1. This suitcase wants to *tell* us other things, too.
2. What does our suitcase want to *say*?
3. The suitcase is *not talking* very loudly to me.
4. The suitcase is *saying* "look at me."
5. It's *telling* us that it is a special suitcase.

***say* = *sagen* leitet die Rede ein oder schließt sie ab**

Sie sagte, sie sei krank.	She said (that) she was ill.
„Was für ein Unsinn", sagte er.	"What nonsense," he said.

***tell* = *mitteilen, anordnen* mit direktem Personenobjekt**

jemandem etwas sagen	tell somebody something
jemandem sagen, was er tun soll	tell somebody what to do

***tell* = *erzählen, sagen* mit abstraktem Objekt**

um die Wahrheit zu sagen	to tell the truth
Witze / Geschichten erzählen	tell jokes / stories

Merke:

tell hat ein Personenobjekt,	*Anne told me (that) she was*
oder ein abstraktes Objekt:	*too tired to tell stories / jokes.*
	Are you telling the truth?
say hat kein direktes Personenobjekt:	*Anne said (that) she was tired.*
Personen werden mit *to* angeschlossen:	*What did he say to you?*

TEST 4: *Past Tense* oder *Present Perfect*?

1. Teacher to pupil: "I never *lied* when I was a child."
   "So when *did* you *start*, Sir?"
2. Did you hear about the Scot who *won* a holiday for two in Majorca? He *went* by himself twice.
3. An intellectual is a man who *has found* something more interesting than women.
4. "I *haven't seen* much of Paul *recently.* Have you?"
   "Yes, I met Paul at the club *recently*."
5. The suitcase is brand new. Somebody *bought* it *recently*.

TEST 5: Sprachfalle *hören* – *listen* oder *hear*?

1. Bernd can't *hear* anything, because he isn't *listening* attentively.
2. He *listened*, but he could only *hear* the ticking of his alarm clock.
3. If you want your wife to *listen*, then talk to another woman.
4. There are only two kinds of executives who fail: those who *listen* to nobody and those who *listen* to everybody.

Merke:
listen: bewusst zu-, hinhören
hear: unbewusst hören, wahrnehmen von Geräuschen

CHAPTER 12

TEST 1: Termine – *appointment, date* oder *deadline*?

Richtig (R) oder Falsch (F)?

		R	F
1.	I've got ~~an appointment~~ *a date* with my girlfriend tonight.		✔
2.	I'd like to make *an appointment* with your doctor.	✔	
3.	Call my secretary and arrange ~~a date~~ *an appointment.*		✔
4.	The ~~appointment~~ *deadline* for applications is 30 April.		✔
5.	Should we set a *date* for the next meeting?	✔	

TEST 2: *Present Perfect Simple* oder *Progressive*?

* *Present Perfect* ist eine Zeit der Gegenwart und steht **nicht** mit Zeitangaben der Vergangenheit.
* *Present Perfect Simple* steht für Zustände und Situationen, die zur Sprechzeit noch andauern.
* *Present Perfect Simple* betont, dass Ergebnisse oder Ereignisse für die Gegenwart wichtig sind.
* *Present Perfect Progressive* betont, dass Vorgänge bis zur Gegenwart <u>ununterbrochen</u> andauern – oft bei Zeiträumen wie *since: seit* mit Zeitpunkt; *for:* seit mit Zeitraum.

1. No woman *has ever shot* / ~~*has ever been shooting*~~ her husband while he was doing the dishes.
2. My wife ~~*has been missed*~~ / *has been missing* for two days. I don't know whether she has left me or gone shopping.
3. An intellectual is a man who *has found* / ~~*has been finding*~~ something more interesting than women.
4. Tina ~~*has taken*~~ / *has been taking* these anti-fat pills for months. Now she's so thin that every time she walks in the park, a dog tries to bury her.

TEST 3: *Present Perfect Simple* oder *Progressive*?

1. Mr Swindler *has owned* the hotel *for two years.*
2. Mr Swindler has *been serving* drinks *all week.*
3. Mr Swindler *has already had* many guests from Germany.
4. You young people *have been working* with the new media *for years.*
5. They *have been sitting* at the computer for an hour.
6. The company *has been operating* in Bournemouth *since 1995.*

TEST 4: Wortschatz-Power. Wie wurde es gesagt?

1.	I won't change my *life* now.	I won't change my *ways* now.
2.	I can't *handle* computers.	I can't *manage with* computers.
3.	Have you any *idea* what computers cost?	Have you any *notion* what computers cost?
4.	Then Bernd has a *brilliant idea.*	Then Bernd has a *brainwave.*

TEST 5: Zeiten-Sprachfallen für Deutsche

	Deutsch	Falsch	Richtig
1.	Ich habe ihn im Bus gesehen.	I *have seen* him on the bus.	I *saw* him on the bus.[1]
2.	Ich habe ein Jahr in Bonn gewohnt.	I *have lived* in Bonn for a year.	I *lived* in Bonn for a year.
3.	Ich wohne seit einem Jahr in Bonn.	I *live* in Bonn *since* a year.	I *have lived* in Bonn *for* a year. / I *have been living* in Bonn for a year.
4.	Wartest du schon lange?	Are *you waiting* (*for*) long?	*Have* you *been waiting* (*for*) long?
5.	Was hast du gesagt?	*What have you said?*	*What did you say?*

CHAPTER 13

TEST 1: Kaufen Sie eine Fahrkarte

Eine Fahrkarte nach London, bitte. — A *ticket* to London, please.
Einfach oder hin und zurück? — Single or *return*?
Zweimal einfach nach Cardiff, bitte. — Two *singles* to Cardiff, please.
Erster oder zweiter Klasse? — *First* or *second* class?

TEST 2: Englisch für den Bahnhof

Der Zug aus X hat eine Verspätung von 15 Minuten. — The train from X *is delayed* by 15 minutes.
Erreiche ich meinen Anschlusszug in X noch? — Will I be able to get my *connection* in X?
Kann ich die Fahrt unterbrechen? — Can I *break* the journey?
Muss ich umsteigen? — Do I have to *change*?
Nein, es ist ein durchgehender Zug. — No, it's a *through* train.
Von welchem Bahnsteig fährt mein Zug ab? — Which *platform* does my train leave from?

1 Die Begegnung *on the bus* muss in der Vergangenheit stattgefunden haben, wenn sich Sprecher und Zuhörer nicht mehr im Bus befinden.

TEST 3: Fragen Sie nach der Abfahrtszeit

Wann fährt der Zug ab? — When does the train *leave*?

Könnten Sie mir ein paar Abfahrtszeiten nennen? — Could you tell me a *few departure* times?

Kommt der Zug pünktlich an? — Will the train be *on time*?

Die Züge fahren jede volle Stunde. — Trains depart *on the hour.*

TEST 4: *Will-Future Simple* oder *Progressive*?

1. *Will* you be *staying there* more than two days?
2. No, we'*ll* only *be* a couple of hours in Bournemouth.
3. *Will* you *be travelling* first or second class, sir?
4. We'*ll take* second class.
5. *Will* you *be paying* cash or by credit card, sir?
6. *Will* you *be coming* back on the same train, sir?

TEST 5: Setzen Sie ins Passiv

1. They stain and dye the leather. — The leather *is stained* and *dyed.*
2. They customise all products. — All products *are customised.*
3. They number the suitcases. — The suitcases *are numbered.*
4. They make every piece by hand. — Every piece *is made by hand.*

TEST 6: Passiv zum Schmunzeln

1. A man who steals a horse *is put* into prison; a man who steals a whole country *is made* king.
2. A pessimist is a man who *has been forced* to live with an optimist.
3. High heels were *invented* by a woman who didn't like to be kissed on her forehead.

CHAPTER 14

TEST 1: Wählen Sie aus! Adjektiv oder Adverb?

1. The gentleman was *clearly* the owner of the shop.
2. Miss Mable tried to keep a *clear* mind.
3. And he looked *shabby.*
4. He was *shabbily* dressed.
5. The gentleman didn't understand *correctly.*
6. His behaviour was *correct.*

Der Unterschied zwischen Adjektiv und Adverb

(Siehe auch key to chapter 10, S. 134)

Das Problem: Die Engländer unterscheiden – wir nicht.

Er ist langsam.	He is slow.
Er isst langsam.	He eats slowly.

Das Adjektiv	Das Adverb
drückt Eigenschaften von Substantiven aus. Es steht a) *vor* dem Substantiv oder b) *nach* bestimmten Verben als Ergänzung. *It smells good etc.*	bestimmt a) Verben (wie geschieht es?) b) Adjektive und Adverbien (wie sehr? / wie viel?)

Bildung des Adverbs: Anhängen von *-ly* an das Adjektiv.

Rechtschreibung: happ*y* → happ**i**ly: -y → I;
true → trul*y*: End-e entfällt;
typ*ic* → typ***ically***: -ic → ically

TEST 2: Wortschatztraining

The verb	And the noun?	
know	*knowledge*	Wissen
presume	*presumption*	Annahme
apologize	*apology*	Entschuldigung

TEST 3: Worte der Entschuldigung

1. *Excuse* me, what time is it, please?
2. I *apologize* for that stupid remark.
3. I'm sure you have some lame *excuses* for not coming.
4. Please accept my sincere *apologies*.

excuse: bevor man jemanden stört
apologise: nachdem man jemanden gestört hat

TEST 4: Müssen – *must, need* oder *have to?*

1. The inspector's name *must* be recorded somewhere.
2. Our detectives will *have to* visit the man in Canterbury.
3. We *need* to know who bought the suitcase.
4. "Do you serve women in this bar?"
   "No, sir, *you must* bring / *have to* bring your own."
5. I *needn't* tell my wife anything. My neighbours do it for me.
6. There are two kinds of men: those we may dream about and those we *must* marry.

must **kann bedeuten:**

a. Zwang, Notwendigkeit	You must bring your own wife.
b. Schlussfolgerung, Gewissheit	Did you see those pictures of the moon? They must have the same gardener we have.
c. Anordnung, Befehl	Rabbi: You must forgive your enemies and repay all your debts. David: Rabbi, I asked you here for spiritual help and you're talking business.

Must hat Ersatzformen zur Bildung von ***Past, Perfect*** und ***Future***

Ersatzform	Zeiten
have (got) to	he had to do it / he has had to do / he will have to do it

TEST 5: Erinnern – *remember* oder *remind?*

1. The old craftsman *remembered* the inspector well.
2. Something *reminded* Bernd of Jenny.
3. I can't *remember* your name, and please don't *remind* me!

Merke: *remember:* sich erinnern
remind someone *of*: jemanden an ... erinnern

TEST 6: Erinnern Sie sich an die Gegenteile?

1. Miss Mable didn't *reject* the apology. She *accepted* it.
2. Maybe Mr Reed is *innocent*, maybe he is *guilty*.
3. Bernd should be more *patient*. He is too *impatient*.

TEST 7: Typisch deutsche Fehler. Korrigieren Sie!

1. There's no *defect* in the workmanship, I hope.
   (*mistakes* passieren aus Unachtsamkeit, *defects* hat man)
2. Is Mr Reed a member of the constabulary?
   (unbestimmter Artikel vor Berufen und Funktionen)
3. A person is innocent until proven guilty, *at least* in England.
   (*at least:* wenigstens; *at last:* letztlich)
4. Miss Mable *has* no son, and has never been married.
   (*have* im Sinne von *besitzen* ist statisch und hat keine Verlaufsform)
5. Bernd was surprised that they could get the information so *easily.*
   (*Adverb* statt *Adjektiv*)

CHAPTER 15

TEST 1: Korrigieren Sie die Fehler in den *Tags*

1. You *found* your shop, *didn't you*?
2. They *didn't want* to give you any information, *did they*?
3. See you tonight. Eight o'clock *will be* okay, *won't it*?
4. Bernd *had done* everything he could to find Heidi, *hadn't he*?

Ergänzen Sie die Tags zum Schmunzeln

5. "Waiter, there's a dead fly in my soup."
   "Well, for 50 pence you don't expect a dead eagle, do you?"
6. The oldest joke we know is when Eve asked Adam, "You love me, *don't you*?" and he replied, "Who else?"

TEST 2: Englisch gegen Geldnot. Ergänzen Sie

Ich habe kein Bargeld mehr.	I have *run* out of cash.
Ich hätte gerne für 500 Euros Britische Pfund.	I'd like to *change* 500 euros into pounds.
Wie ist der Wechselkurs heute?	What's the *rate* today?
Wo ist bitte der Geldautomat?	Where is the *cash* dispenser?
Kann ich Bargeld mit meiner Kreditkarte abheben?	Can I *draw* cash with my credit card?

TEST 3: Probleme am Geldautomaten

Der Automat hat meine Karte einbehalten.	The machine's *taken* my card.
Haben Sie die richtige Geheimnummer eingegeben?	*Did* you *type* in the correct pin?
Ich fürchte, Sie haben Ihr Konto überzogen.	I'm afraid you'*ve overdrawn* your account.
Ich habe meine Kreditkarte verloren. Was soll ich tun?	I'*ve lost* my credit card. What shall I do?
Sollen wir Ihr Konto sperren?	*Shall* we *bar* your account?

CHAPTER 16

TEST 1: Übersetzen Sie. Adjektiv oder Adverb?

1. Bernd *quickly* drops into Mucks&Spunsers.
2. He wants to look *normal.*
3. Five minutes later Bernd comes out *happily*.
4. He is *happy* to have found the right outfit for the date.
5. The new clothes fit *perfectly.*

TEST 2: English for the clothes shop

Werden Sie schon bedient?	Are you being *served*?
Könnten Sie mir vielleicht helfen?	I *wonder* if you could help me.
Was für eine Größe brauchen Sie?	What size do you *take*?
Ich fürchte, dieser Anzug sitzt nicht gut.	I'm afraid the suit doesn't *fit* me very well.
Man kann es ändern, ohne Aufpreis.	It can be *altered* at no extra charge.
Diese Bluse passt gut zu Ihrem Rock.	This blouse goes *nicely* with your skirt.
Ich brauche die nächste Größe.	I need the next *size.*

TEST 3: English for dinner

Herr Ober! Ich hätte gerne die Speisekarte.	Excuse me, *waiter,* could I have the menu, please?
Haben Sie schon gewählt?	Are you ready to *order*?
Womit wollen Sie anfangen?	What would you like to *start* with?

Ich nehme die Suppe.	I'll *take* the soup.
Und danach?	And to *follow*?
Ich versuche mal das Lamm.	I'll *try* the lamb.
Was möchten Sie trinken?	What would you *like* to drink?
Ein kleines Helles.	A half of *lager*, please.
Ich möchte bitte zahlen.	Could I have the *bill*, please?

TEST 4: Noch einmal: Adjektiv oder Adverb?

1. He sleeps *well* that night.
2. He has a *good* night's sleep.
3. Bernd is *eager* to see Jenny again.
4. He *eagerly* looks forward to his date.
5. He feels really *good* when he is with Jenny.
6. I thinks the breast of duck sounds *good.*

TEST 5: Sprachfallen: *eventual* heißt nicht *eventuell*

1. We have made a plan in order to avoid *possible* difficulties.
2. She *eventually* passed her driving test.
3. Our *eventual* aim is to find a drug against cancer.
4. My company will *possibly* use your service very often.

CHAPTER 17

TEST 1: Deutsch: *wenn* – Englisch: *if* oder *when*?

1. Tact is the art of saying nothing *when* there is nothing to say.
2. *If* you look like your passport photo you really need the holiday.
3. Why does a Lada have heated rear windscreens?
   To keep your hands warm *when* you push it.
4. Don't tell lies, *if* you can use statistics.
5. My wife says she'll leave me, *if* I don't throw out my computer. I'll miss her.

when ist ein zeitliches „immer wenn / dann wenn";
if ist ein „bedingendes wenn", es kann oft durch „falls" ersetzt werden.

TEST 2: *for* oder *since*?

1. Nothing has been heard of Heidi *since* she was kidnapped.
2. Patient: Aren't these pills habit-forming?
   Doctor: Rubbish, I've been taking them *for* years.
3. I have been in love with the same woman *for* forty years. If my wife finds out she'll kill me.

TEST 3: Es muss nicht immer *Present Perfect* sein

1. We *were married* successfully *for* four years. Then my wife *lost* her job.
2. I *haven't been* so upset *since* Margaret *asked* me what I wanted to name the baby. Margaret – that's my secretary.

Situationen, die in der Vergangenheit begonnen haben und bis zum Zeitpunkt des Sprechens andauern, werden mit dem *Present Perfect* ausgedrückt. Im Deutschen steht oft Gegenwart.

➤ **Achtung:**
Er wohnt *seit* drei Jahren in Bonn. He *has lived* in Bonn *for* three years (*for three years* + Perfekt: seit drei Jahren).

Er hat drei Jahre lang in Bonn gewohnt. He lived in Bonn *for* three years (*for three years* + Vergangenheit: drei Jahre lang).

Vorsicht: Einleitendes *since* kann auch *da ja* bedeuten.

TEST 4: If-Sätze Typ I – Wie steht's mit den Verbformen?

1. If we *look* back to the beginning of the book we *will find* a "happy" couple coming to England on holiday.
2. If Black *loses* the bag again the Captain *will stick* his feet into a block of concrete.
3. If Black *leaves* Heidi there, the police *will get* information from her.
4. What *will* the Captain *say* if he *brings* the girl to the safe house?

Typ I: Erfüllbare Bedingungen

1. Im *If-Satz* steht eine Zeit der Gegenwart, also Present oder Present Perfect. Im *If-Satz* steht ***kein Will-Future***!
2. Im Hauptsatz steht eine Verbform, die Sinn macht: z. B. Present Perfect oder Will-Future, Imperativ oder modales Hilfsverb wie *can, could, may* etc.

	If-Satz: erfüllbare Bedingung	Hauptsatz: die Folgen
a.	If you *want* your wife to listen,	*talk* to another woman.
	Hauptsatz: die Folgen	**If-Satz: erfüllbare Bedingung**
b.	Life begins at 40, but you *could miss* a lot	if you *wait* till then.

TEST 5: Können Sie steigern?

1. Suppliers are coming *earlier and earlier.*
2. The kidnapping ran *more* or *less* like this.
3. Bernd did *his best* to find Heidi.

TEST 6: Setzen Sie ins Passiv

1. Heidi *was sprayed* with something *by Black.*
2. Heidi *was kidnapped by Black.*
3. Bernd *was assisted by Miss Mable.*
4. The Captain *was being helped* by his nephew.

TEST 7: If-Sätze Typ II – Wie steht's mit den Verbformen?

1. If Heidi *knew* what was in the bag she *would be* in the Bahamas by now.
2. If Black *lost* the bag again the Captain *would stick* his feet into a block of concrete.
3. If Black *left* her there, the police *would get* information from her.

Typ II: Nicht oder kaum erfüllbare Bedingungen

If-Satz: Bedingung	Hauptsatz: mögliche Folgen
If the Sahara *belonged* to Russia,	within three months there *wouldn't be* any sand left.

* Im If-Satz steht *Past Tense* und nicht Konditional wie im Deutschen.
* Im Hauptsatz kann modales Hilfsverb *would, could, might* + Infinitiv stehen.

➤ **Achtung!**

* Mit Typ II spricht man nicht über die Vergangenheit, sondern über die Gegenwart (nicht erfüllbare Bedingung) oder Zukunft (theoretisch oder nur schwer erfüllbare Bedingung).

* **If** kann auch *ob* bedeuten und eine indirekte Frage einleiten. That's a nice hat you are wearing. I wonder *if* the style will ever come back

TEST 8: If-Sätze: Typ I und Typ II

1. Mum: Dad, please take Jimmy to the zoo today.
   Dad: Not me! *If the zoo wants him*, they *can come* and get him!
2. More husbands *would* leave home *if they knew* how to pack their suitcases.
3. Doctor: If I find it necessary to operate, *will you be able* to pay for it?
   Patient: *If I didn't have the money, would* you find it necessary to operate?

CHAPTER 18

TEST 1: Wechseln Sie die Wortart

He said it with a sweet *smile.*
He said it with a *dangerous* smile.
It's *probable* that she's seen you.
Sam did it with *extreme care.*

He said it and smiled *sweetly.*
He smiled *dangerously.*
She's *probably* seen you.
Sam did it *extremely carefully.*

TEST 2: Welches ist das passende *Question Tag*?

1. Let me in, **A.** *will you*? (Aufforderung an andere Personen)
2. Let's talk about it, **B.** *shall we*? (Aufforderung, Vorschlag; man bezieht sich mit ein)
3. He stole the bag while she was out, **B.** *didn't he*? (Vollverben werden durch *do* bzw. *did* ersetzt)
4. I'm stupid, **B.** *aren't I*? (Merken Sie sich diesen Sonderfall)
5. We'll have to kill the girl, **A.** *won't we*? (Hilfsverben werden im *Tag* wiederholt)

TEST 3: Wie steht es mit den kleinen Wörtern?

1. A girl picked *up* my suitcase.
2. She took the suitcase *by* mistake.
3. I managed to get hold *of* her address.
4. Get *to* the point, Sam.
5. I'm intrigued how you pulled it *off.*
6. Now Blake spoke *up.*

TEST 4: Verbformen im Bedingungssatz Typ III

1. If Sam *hadn't arrived*, the Captain *would have driven* to his place.
2. If I *had known* the complications, I *wouldn't have sent* you.
3. If Christopher Columbus *had not discovered* America, he *would have saved* us a lot of trouble.
4. If Goethe *had used* a computer, he *might have erased* Faust.

Bedingungssatz Typ III:

Nicht mehr erfüllbare Bedingungen

Hauptsatz: Folgen	If-Satz: Bedingung
Eve was unhappy in Paradise because she couldn't tell Adam about all the wonderful lovers she *could /would have had*	if she *hadn't married* him.

1. Im If-Satz steht Past Perfect (she *hadn't married* him) und nicht das Konditional wie im Deutschen.
2. Im Hauptsatz steht Konditional II: *would have* + Partizip Perfekt oder *would / might / could* + *have* + Partizip Perfekt.

TEST 5: Was bedeutet das einfache *Will-Future*?

A. Voraussage B. Vermutung, Annahme C. Versprechen

1. The police *will force* her to talk. A
2. Well, we *will have to* kill her, won't we? B
3. I'm sure she *won't tell* them anything. B
4. Don't worry. Let me handle it. I *will take care* of her. C

TEST 6: Was bedeutet das *Will-Future Progressive*?

A. Höflichkeit B. nicht abgeschlossene Situation in der Zukunft
C. geplante oder automatische Folgehandlung

1. And sooner or later Heidi *will be talking* to the police. C
2. *Will you be staying* another night, sir? A
3. Let me post this letter for you. On my way home I'*ll be passing* the post office anyway. C
4. When you read this picture postcard I'll be lying on the beach in Florida. B
5. *Will* you still *be sending* me Valentines when I'm sixty-four? B
6. *Will* you *be paying* by credit card? A

CHAPTER 19

TEST 1: Indirekte Rede: Korrigieren Sie die Fehler

1. Tina *thought* Robinson Crusoe ~~is~~ *was* a world famous tenor.
2. The first time Tina ever saw a cow she thought it ~~is~~ *was* a bull that ~~has~~ *had* swallowed a glove.
3. Bob told the mechanic to fill up the petrol tank. He thought that ~~will~~ *would* double the price of his Trabi.

TEST 2: Übersetzen Sie die deutschen Klammern

1. The Captain *told* the men that *he had* a friend in Canterbury.
2. He *said he was going* to kill Heidi.
3. Blake *thought he had known* what he was getting into.

TEST 3: Entscheiden Sie: Adjektiv oder Adverb?

1. Blake didn't feel *happy* with the Captain and Sam.
2. The two talked and talked and got on *well* together.
3. The Captain smiled *pleasantly.*
4. The *pleasant* young Blake wanted to help Heidi.

TEST 4: Was ist gemeint?

1. Blake *takes care of* the prisoner. — **B.** bewachen
2. Blake went to *look after* Heidi. — **A.** sehen nach
3. The Captain will *deal with* her. — **A.** töten

TEST 5: Blake berichtet, was man ihm erzählt hat

1. The Captain *told* me (that) *I could earn* a bit of extra money.
2. He explained that *he was getting back* his diamonds.
3. He told me he *would deal* with the girl at the weekend.
4. Heidi told me that she *had picked up* the wrong suitcase.

CHAPTER 20

TEST 1: Das Gerund steht nach Präpositionen

1. Miss Mable is *keen on visiting* Inspector Reed.
2. She is *interested in meeting* the inspector.
3. They have *difficulty in breaking* into Reed's house.
4. Tact is the *art of saying nothing* when there is nothing to say.

TEST 2: Haben Sie Sprachgefühl? Gerund oder Infinitiv?

1. You needn't *expect* a good cup of coffee in Hastings.
   (Infinitiv nach modalen Hilfsverben wie *can, must, may* etc.)
2. I can't *risk losing* money when customers forget to pay.
3. They took a taxi to avoid *arriving* in the dark.
4. The first man *to tear* a telephone book probably had teenage kids.
   (Infinitiv nach Superlativen)

Verben, nach denen Gerund steht

avoid	*vermeiden*	Avoid driving in the rush-hour.
consider	*erwägen*	We are considering going to France.
deny	*leugnen*	He denied knowing anything about it.
enjoy	*genießen*	She enjoys playing tennis.
excuse	*entschuldigen*	Excuse my interrupting you.
finish	*beenden*	You should finish reading this book.
imagine	*sich vorstellen*	I can't imagine living anywhere else.
postpone	*verschieben*	Let's postpone making a decision.
practise	*üben*	Practise playing the piano every day.
risk	*riskieren*	I can't risk losing money.
suggest	*vorschlagen*	He suggested going to the zoo.

TEST 3: Sprachfalle *use*

1. As a boy Bernd *used to climb* trees and fences. **B**
   Er kletterte *früher* ...
2. But he is not *used to breaking* into someone else's house. **C**
   Er ist es nicht gewöhnt zu ...
3. Mr Swindler always *uses* one *teabag* for two people. **A**
   Er verwendet ...
4. I *used to be* a werewolf, but I'm alright noooooow. **B**
   Ich war früher ...

5. I *used to be* arrogant. Now I'm perfectly okay. Ich war früher ... — B
6. It's no *use crying* over spilled milk. Es hat keinen Zweck zu ... — D

TEST 4: Infinitiv oder Gerund? Richtig oder falsch?

	R	F
1. The art of medicine *consists in amusing* the patient while nature cures the disease.	✔	
2. My *way ~~to joke~~ of joking* is to tell the truth.		✔
3. Psychiatrist: Do you have *difficulty in making* up your mind? Patient: Well, yes and no.	✔	
4. A diplomat is a man who can tell you to go to hell in such a way that you actually look *forward to ~~go~~ going* on the trip		✔
5. Clarity is the ability to give directions *without taking* your hands out of your pockets.	✔	

CHAPTER 21

TEST 1: Was Polizisten so fragen

1. In welchem Hotel wohnen Sie?	Which hotel are you staying at?
2. Seit wann sind Sie in England?	How long have you been in England?
3. Wann sind Sie geboren?	When were you born?
4. Wo sind Sie geboren?	Where were you born?
5. Wo ist Ihr ständiger Wohnsitz?	What's your permanent address / residence?

Zu 4. und 5.: Da die Geburt in der Vergangenheit abgeschlossen wurde, steht im Englischen *Past Tense.*

TEST 2: Wie steht es im Ausweis?

Date of *birth:*	08.03.1977
Place of *birth*:	Heidelberg
Nationality:	German
Residence:	Heidelberg
Colour of *eyes:*	blue
Signature of *bearer:*	Bernd Bubel
Height:	182 cm

TEST 3: Richtig oder falsch – Infinitiv oder Gerund?

		R	F
1.	Then the sergeant *decides to* interview Bernd.		✔
2.	Bernd *denies stealing* anything.	✔	
3.	He doesn't *risk telling* lies to the sergeant.		✔
4.	Was it worth *ruining* his clothes for?		✔
5.	Miss Mable says she has come *to visit* her nephew.	✔	
6.	But he doesn't appear *to live* there any more.		✔
7.	Perhaps the postman can help you *to find* him.	✔	

Prägen Sie sich einige Verben ein, die Infinitiv mit *to* haben.

Wünschen, wollen, Bedürfnis	Zulassen, veranlassen
I want to leave	allow someone to stay
I wish to stay	cause someone to leave
I need to talk	tell someone to do
I intend to do	agree to someone to do
I hope to see you	promise someone to wait
I refuse to go	decide to buy

TEST 4: Nicht verwechseln – *near, nearest, next, nearby*

1. Miss Mable asked the policeman to drop them off at the *nearest* post-office.
2. "How come you were born in Iowa?" – "I wanted to be *near* my mother."
3. Mike was asked what his favourite drink was. "The *next* one," he replied.
4. Excuse me, where is the *nearest* toilet? It's urgent.

next **= nächste in (zeitlicher / räumlicher) Reihenfolge**	
Wer ist der Nächste?	Who's next?
das nächste Mal	next time

near, nearer, nearest **(örtlich) = nahe, näher, nächstgelegen**	
in der Nähe von Hastings	near Hastings
der nächstgelegene Supermarkt	the nearest supermarket

TEST 5: Übersetzen Sie. Auf die Stellung kommt es an

1. He wanted to marry ***her***. — *Er wollte **sie** heiraten.*
2. He wanted ***her*** to marry. — *Er wollte, **dass sie** heiratet.*
3. He wanted ***her*** to marry ***him***. — *Er wollte, **dass sie ihn** heiratet.*

CHAPTER 22

TEST 1: Drei verschiedene Verben für *annehmen*

1. Miss Mable *accepted* the policeman's offer.
2. Miss Mable *presumed* the day's events have made Bernd nervous.
3. I *suppose* Mr Swindler will be frustrated.

TEST 2: Setzen Sie in das *Simple Past*

1. The police car *sped* them across country to Hastings.
   (speed, sped, sped)
2. Blake *heard* a voice outside.
   (hear, heard, heard)
3. He *blew* the candle out.
   (blow, blew, blown)
4. Swindler *threw* a tantrum.
   (throw, threw, thrown)

TEST 3: Je kürzer das Wort, desto schwieriger

1. Blake tied Heidi *up* again.
2. A car drove *off*.
3. They trespassed *on* other people's property.
4. They were wondering *about* the drinks.
5. What were you thinking *of*, Bernd? – Was ist in dich gefahren?
   What were you thinking *about*, Bernd? – Worüber hast du nachgedacht?

TEST 4: In der Kürze liegt die Würze

1. It's been a day *not to be forgotten*.
2. It's been a *day to remember*.
3. The police car *arrived making* a terrible noise.
4. The police, *trying to be friendly*, bundled them into a police car.
5. Blake sat down in the chair *banging* his knee on the table.

CHAPTER 23

TEST 1: Wie übersetzt man *wie*?

1. Do it *as* quickly *as* you can.
2. Blake's brain was working *like* a whirlwind.
3. We'll do it *as* planned.
4. *How* is the Captain?
5. *What* is the Captain like?

TEST 2: Nicht verwechseln! Übersetzen Sie!

Blake waited *for ten minutes.*	Wartete zehn Minuten *lang.*
Blake has waited *for ten minutes.*	Wartet *seit* zehn Minuten.
How is Tom?	*Wie geht es* Tom?
What is Tom like?	*Wie ist* Tom (so)?

TEST 3: Nicht verwechseln!

1. Heidi began to get *quite* cold. (ganz kalt)
2. The drug will keep Heidi *quiet.* (ruhig stellen)
3. *Then* he heard the noise of the diesel truck. (dann)
4. Don't let your superiors know you're better *than* they are. (als)
5. There was *somebody* in the house. (jemand, bejaht)
6. But the police thought there wasn't *anybody* in the house. (jemand, verneint)

TEST 4: Erinnern Sie sich an den Wortlaut im Text?

1.	the *positive aspect* of a situation	the *upside* of a situation
2.	the *negative aspect* of a situation	the *downside* of a situation
3.	*kill someone*	*do* someone *in*
4.	*tidy up* the house	*clear up* the house

TEST 5: Noch mal das Wörtchen *wie*

Satz 1, 2, 3 sind falsch.

1. Blake felt a cold *shiver run* down his back.
2. Just then they heard Sam's key turn in the door.
3. A woman who wants to be *like* a man has no ambition.
4. Etiquette is knowing *how* to yawn with your mouth closed.

zu 1. und 2:
Nach den **Verben der sinnlichen Wahrnehmung** (*see, feel, hear* etc.) steht Infinitiv ohne *to* oder *-ing*-Form. Das *wie* wird nicht übersetzt: *Ich sah, wie er das Geld nahm.* I saw him take / taking the money.
zu 3: *like* vergleicht Substantive, *as* Verben und Adjektive.
zu 4: Nach Fragewörtern steht Infinitiv mit *to.*

TEST 6: *our, us* oder *ourselves*?

1. Let *us* make a plan.
2. We'll have to bring forward *our* plans.
3. The downside is that they've found out about *us.*
4. We have to organize this properly, or we'll give *ourselves* away.

CHAPTER 24

TEST 1: Bilden Sie die Verlaufsform des *Will-Future*

1. The Captain *will be barging in* on us soon.
2. Where *will* you *be going* after we leave Brighton?
3. *Will* you *be staying* long, or is it another flying visit?

Das Will-Future Progressive drückt aus, dass sich etwas *ohnehin, sowieso, zwangsläufig, wie geplant* oder *weil es so üblich ist* ereignen wird.	We *will be landing* at Heathrow in 15 minutes. You needn't send Paul a fax. You'*ll be meeting* him at the conference tomorrow, remember?

TEST 2: Bilden Sie das *Going to-Future*

1. The Captain *is going to barge in* on us soon.
2. Where are you *going (to go)* after we leave Brighton?
3. Are you *going to stay long*, or is it just a flying visit?

Going to-Future steht für	
a) Pläne, Vorhaben und Absichten	Voice on telephone: Give us $50,000 or you won't see your wife again. Scotsman: I'm *not going to* give you the money. But I'm interested in your offer.
b) Schlussfolgerung aufgrund vorhandener Anzeichen	Our son *is going to* be an auctioneer. This is the third valuable vase he has brought under the hammer.

TEST 3: Bilden Sie das einfache *Will-Future*

1. It'*ll be* about 8:30 *p.m.* when they arrive at the hotel.
2. The chances are that Bernd *will* not *be* at the hotel.
3. The diamonds *will help* our heroes to go underground.

Will-Future steht für

a) Voraussagen	Drinking *will not* stop your problems, but it will give you lots of interesting new ones.
b) Vermutungen	
c) Versprechen	Father: I *will give* a handsome prize to the man who marries my daughter. Young man: Can I see the prize first, sir?

TEST 4: Korrigieren Sie die Fehler

1. I left my suitcase at the accident ward a week ago. (Ort vor Zeit)
2. Please ~~bring~~ take us to Dover Bus Station. (*bring:* Bewegung zum Sprecher hin; *take:* vom Sprecher weg)
3. ~~Why~~ What are you doing that for? oder *Why* are you doing that ~~for~~?
4. Blake moved ~~as~~ *like* a flash of lightning.

TEST 5: Wohin mit dem Adverb?

1. Blake *carefully* poured whisky into Sam's mouth.
2. Blake *quickly* got the number of the ward.
3. Then Heidi *boldly* walked into the hotel.
4. You *certainly* don't remember where your room is, do you?
5. To err is human but to *really* foul things up you need a computer.

Das Adverb der Art und Weise steht in der Regel (wenn nicht besonders betont) vor dem zugehörigen Verb.

TEST 6: Übersetzen Sie

1. Sam sat upright.	Sam *saß* aufrecht / gerade.
2. Blake sat Sam upright.	Blake *setze* Sam aufrecht hin.
3. You'd better give me another whisky.	Gib mir *lieber noch einen* Whisky.
4. They had a cup of tea.	Sie tranken eine Tasse Tee.

CHAPTER 25

TEST 1: Glückssache: *luck, be lucky* oder *be happy*?

1. Heidi was *lucky* (that) Bernd was out. But she wasn't *happy.*
2. Tom is *lucky.* He has got a wife and a car, and they both work.
3. Best wishes for a *happy* and successful first marriage.
4. Success is just a matter of *luck.* Ask a failure.

TEST 2: Vier Verben – acht Partizipien

1. Swindler thought he had *interesting* news.
   But Mable was not *interested.*
2. Swindler thought he was *amusing.*
   But Miss Mable was not *amused.*
3. Bernd is too *tired* to listen to.
   Swindler's *tiring* experience of the world.
4. Blake was *excited* when he found Heidi half-naked.
   "What an *exciting* girl!" he thought.

TEST 3: Partizipien verkürzen Nebensätze

1. (*While*) serving the drinks *Swindler* began to giggle.
2. *Entering* the room *the Captain* smelt alcohol.
3. He looked down at Sam *his face darkening.*
4. An oyster is a fish *built* like a nut.
5. The serious music lover is the type who, *when hearing* a soprano in the bathroom, puts his ear to the keyhole.

1. Mit Partizipien verkürzt man notwendige Relativsätze. Relativpronomen und Formen von *to be* werden weglassen.
2. Partizipien verkürzen auch adverbiale Nebensätze, die sagen, *was wann, wie, warum, womit* geschieht oder geschehen ist. Konjunktionen (z.B. *while*) können bei Verkürzung wegfallen.

TEST 4: Sagen Sie es mit ähnlichen Worten

There was no *answer.* — There was no *reply.*
Time to *leave the* ship. — Time to *abandon ship.*
He *hurried* back. — He *rushed* back.
I *guess* they have disappeared. — I *suppose* they have gone.

TEST 5: Was versteckt sich hinter *'s*?

1. *Heidi's* had a fit of conscience. — Heidi *has* had ...
2. Oh, *that's* good of you. — That *is* good ...
3. *Let's* go back to the safe-house. — Let *us* go ...
4. *It's* all happened so quickly. — It *has* happened ...
5. *Sam's* bloody well drunk. — Sam *is* ...
6. *He's* risked the whole operation. — He *has* risked ...
7. *There's* been a change of plan. — There *has* been ...

TEST 6: Ergänzen Sie die Indirekte Rede

1. Somebody's after me.
   Heidi told Swindler (that) somebody *was* after *her.*
2. Where's the foreign girl?
   Dick asked where the foreign girl *was.*
3. There's been a change of plan.
   He told Dick (that) there *had been* a change of plan.
4. Sam's risked the whole plan.
   The Captain feared (that) Sam *had risked* the whole plan.

CHAPTER 26

TEST 1: Wie lautet die Passivform?

1. They blocked the road. — The road *was blocked.*
2. They forced the car to stop. — The car was *forced* to stop.
3. They had tied Heidi up. — Heidi *had been tied* up.
4. They had cut the rope. — The rope *had been cut.*
5. They had *snuffed out* the candle. — The candle *had been snuffed out.*
6. They were enjoying alcohol. — Alcohol *was being enjoyed.*

Siehe auch key to chapter 8, Seite 34

TEST 2: Was ist das Gegenteil der kursiven Worte?

1. A car began to *pull out* down the road. — *pull in*
2. Jenny is turning out to be *reliable.* — *unreliable*
3. The mobile phone is most *useful.* — *useless*
4. They *lighted* a candle. — *snuffed out*

TEST 3: Ergänzen Sie die Verbformen

1. Customer, at a repair shop: Please change the oil.
   Mechanic: If I were you, I *would keep* the oil and change the car.
2. My wife says she *will leave* me if I don't throw out my computer. I will miss her.

TEST 4: Intelligentes Raten

3	Release the handbrake.	*Handbremse*
7	Press the accelerator, drive away.	*Gaspedal*
1	Put the key into the ignition.	*Zündschloss*
5	Put the car into first gear.	*Gang*
6	Release the clutch very slowly.	*loslassen*
4	Push in the clutch.	*treten*
2	Turn it and start the engine.	*Motor*

TEST 5: Streichen Sie den falschen Ausdruck

1. I have *borrowed* / ~~*lent*~~ Jenny's mobile to help in emergencies.
2. Jenny ~~*borrowed*~~ / *lent* me her mobile to help in emergencies.
3. Let's go to the ~~*next*~~ / *nearest* telephone box.
4. The phone's out of order. Let's try the *next* / ~~*nearest*~~ phone-box.
5. We *needn't* / ~~*mustn't*~~ search for a phone-box. I've got a mobile.
   We mustn't / must not = *Wir dürfen nicht*
6. May I ~~*remember*~~ / *remind* you of a few items I mentioned before.
7. You'll *remember* / ~~*remind*~~ me, sergeant, won't you?

CHAPTER 27

TEST 1: Verbinden Sie die Sätze durch *ing*-Formen

1. The sergeant sprang backwards *looking* at the gun.
2. She stuck her umbrella through the window *opening* it out like an airbag.
3. Heidi phoned yesterday *wanting* to know where the suitcase was.

Der Platz der Adverbien im Satz

A. Vor dem Vollverb bzw. zwischen erstem Hilfs- und Vollverb stehen

1. Adverbien der unbestimmten Zeit (*now, still, later, soon, already, just*, **Test 2**: 2, 3, 4, **Test 4**: Satz 6)
2. Adverbien der unbestimmten Häufigkeit (*always, never*) (Test 4, Sätze 1 – 6)
3. Adverbien, die einen Grad ausdrücken (*only, quite*, **Test 2**: Satz 1)

➤ **Achtung**

Diese Adverbien stehen nach einer Form von *be* (*is, was, were*) wenn es Vollverb ist. (**Test 2**: 5)

B. Hinter dem Verb, das sie bestimmen, stehen

Adverbien der Art und Weise

My husband and I had lived *happily* for many years – then we met.

C. Am Ende oder am Anfang des Satzes stehen

Adverbien des Ortes und der bestimmten Zeit (*last night, today, tomorrow, tonight*) stehen am Ende (oder Anfang) des Satzes. (*yesterday*, **Test 2**: 6.)

TEST 2: Wohin mit den Adverbien?

1. You *nearly* ran into me.
2. He was *already* winding down his window.
3. I've *just* had a holiday in the Lake District.
4. I *just* got through to Jenny at the hospital.
5. Oh, it's *only* you, Miss Mable.
6. The flying foreigner was here *yesterday*.

TEST 3: Wie übersetzt man *lassen*?

1. The sergeant *phoned for* a prison car. (*kommen lassen*)
2. Heidi *let* him *know* that she was okay. (*wissen lassen*)
3. She *left* a message for room six. (*hinterlassen*).
4. Swindler *made* Heidi *pay* her bill before he *let* her *have* her passport. (*hinterlassen, überlassen*).

5. On holiday, people drive thousands of miles just to *have* their picture *taken* in front of their cars. (*machen lassen*)

TEST 4: Wo ist der Platz des Adverbs?

1. A wise husband *never* laughs at his wife's old clothes.
2. A husband's last words are *always*, "Okay, buy it."
3. I surprised my wife with a mink coat. She'd *never* seen me in one.
4. I *always* arrive late at the office, but I make up for it by leaving early.
5. Some errors will *always* go unnoticed until the book is in print.
6. God would *never* have given us the bicycle, if he had wanted us to walk.

a complete list of **irregular verbs**

Die mit * markierten Verben haben auch eine regelmäßige Form, d. h. Past (Spalte 2) und Participle (Spalte 3) enden auf *ed*.

Infinitive	**Past Simple**	**Past Participle** *(für Perfect und Passive)*	***German***
arise	arose	arisen	*entstehen*
awake	awoke	awoken	*aufwachen*
be	was/were	been	*sein*
beat	beat	beat	*schlagen*
become	became	become	*werden*
begin	began	begun	*beginnen*
bend	bent	bent	*biegen*
bet*	bet	bet	*wetten*
bid	bid	bid	*bieten*
bind	bound	bound	*binden*
bite	bit	bitten	*beißen*
bleed	bled	bled	*bluten*
blow	blew	blown	*blasen*
break	broke	broken	*brechen*
breed	bred	bred	*brüten / züchten*
bring	brought	brought	*bringen*
broadcast	broadcast	broadcast	*senden / übertragen (Rundfunk)*
build	built	built	*bauen*
burn*	burnt	burnt	*brennen*
burst	burst	burst	*bersten*
buy	bought	bought	*kaufen*
catch	caught	caught	*fangen*
choose	chose	chosen	*wählen*

cling	clung	clung	*sich klammern an*
come	came	come	*kommen*
cost	cost	cost	*kosten*
creep	crept	crept	*kriechen*
cut	cut	cut	*schneiden*
deal	dealt	dealt	*handeln*
dig	dug	dug	*graben*
do	did	done	*tun*
draw	drew	drawn	*ziehen / zeichnen*
dream*	dreamt	dreamt	*träumen*
drink	drank	drunk	*trinken*
drive	drove	driven	*fahren*
eat	ate	eaten	*essen*
fall	fell	fallen	*fallen*
feed	fed	fed	*füttern*
feel	felt	felt	*fühlen*
fight	fought	fought	*kämpfen*
find	found	found	*finden*
fling	flung	flung	*schleudern*
fly	flew	flown	*fliegen*
forbid	forbade / forbad	forbidden	*verbieten*
forecast	forecast	forecast	*vorhersagen*
forget	forgot	forgotten	*vergessen*
forgive	forgave	forgiven	*vergeben*
freeze	froze	frozen	*frieren*
get	got	got	*bekommen*
give	gave	given	*geben*
go	went	gone (been to)	*gehen*
grind	ground	ground	*schleifen*
grow	grew	grown	*wachsen*
hang*	hung	hung	*aufhängen*
have	had	had	*haben*
hear	heard	heard	*hören*
hide	hid	hidden	*verstecken*
hit	hit	hit	*treffen*
hold	held	held	*halten*
hurt	hurt	hurt	*verletzen*

keep	kept	kept	*behalten*
kneel*	knelt	knelt	*knien*
knit*	knit	knit	*stricken*
know	knew	known	*wissen / kennen*
lay	laid	laid	*legen*
lead	led	led	*führen*
lean*	leant	leant	*lehnen*
leap*	leapt	leapt	*springen*
learn*	learnt	learnt	*lernen*
leave	left	left	*verlassen*
lend	lent	lent	*(ver-)leihen*
let	let	let	*lassen*
lie	lay	lain	*liegen*
light*	lit	lit	*anzünden*
lose	lost	lost	*verlieren*
make	made	made	*machen*
mean	meant	meant	*bedeuten*
meet	met	met	*treffen*
mistake	mistook	mistaken	*verwechseln*
misunderstand	misunderstood	misunderstood	*missverstehen*
mow	mowed	mown	*mähen*
overcome	overcame	overcome	*überwinden*
pay	paid	paid	*(be-)zahlen*
put	put	put	*(hin-)legen*
quit*	quit	quit	*aufgeben / kündigen*
read	read	read	*lesen*
rid	rid	rid	*befreien, loswerden*
ride	rode	ridden	*reiten*
ring	rang	rung	*läuten*
rise	rose	risen	*sich erheben, aufstehen*
run	ran	run	*laufen*
saw	sawed	sawn	*sägen*
say	said	said	*sagen*
see	saw	seen	*sehen*
seek	sought	sought	*suchen*
sell	sold	sold	*verkaufen*
send	sent	sent	*(ver-)senden*

set	set	set	*setzen / stellen / legen*
sew	sewed	sewn	*nähen*
shake	shook	shaken	*zittern*
shed	shed	shed	*verschütten*
shine	shone	shone	*scheinen*
shoot	shot	shot	*schießen*
show	showed	shown	*zeigen*
shrink	shrank	shrunk	*schrumpfen*
shut	shut	shut	*schließen*
sing	sang	sung	*singen*
sink	sank	sunk	*sinken*
sit	sat	sat	*sitzen*
sleep	slept	slept	*schlafen*
slide	slid	slid	*gleiten*
sling	slung	slung	*schleudern*
slink	slunk	slunk	*schleichen*
slit	slit	slit	*aufschlitzen*
smell*	smelt	smelt	*riechen*
sow	sowed	sown	*säen*
speak	spoke	spoken	*sprechen*
speed*	sped	sped	*beschleunigen*
spell*	spelt	spelt	*buchstabieren*
spend	spent	spent	*ausgeben*
spill*	spilt	spilt	*verschütten*
spin	spun/span	spun	*spinnen*
spit	spat	spat	*spucken*
split	split	split	*spalten*
spoil*	spoilt	spoilt	*verderben*
spread	spread	spread	*verbreiten*
spring	sprang	sprung	*springen*
stand	stood	stood	*stehen*
steal	stole	stolen	*stehlen*
stick	stuck	stuck	*stecken*
sting	stung	stung	*stechen*
stink	stank	stunk	*stinken*
stride	strode	stridden	*schreiten*
strike	struck	struck	*schlagen*

string	strung	strung	*spannen, zubinden*
strive	strove	striven	*streben*
swear	swore	sworn	*schwören*
sweat*	sweat	sweat	*schwitzen*
sweep	swept	swept	*kehren*
swell	swelled	swollen	*anschwellen*
swim	swam	swum	*schwimmen*
swing	swung	swung	*schwingen*
take	took	taken	*nehmen*
teach	taught	taught	*lehren*
tear	tore	torn	*reißen*
tell	told	told	*sagen, erzählen*
think	thought	thought	*denken*
throw	threw	thrown	*werfen*
thrust	thrust	thrust	*stoßen*
tread	trod	trodden	*treten*
understand	understood	understood	*verstehen*
undertake	undertook	undertaken	*übernehmen*
upset	upset	upset	*umwerfen*
wake	woke	woken	*wachen*
wear	wore	worn	*tragen, anhaben*
weave	wove	woven	*weben*
weep	wept	wept	*weinen*
wet	wet	wet	*nass machen*
win	won	won	*gewinnen*
wind	wound	wound	*winden, wickeln*
withdraw	withdrew	withdrawn	*zurückziehen*
withhold	withheld	withheld	*zurückhalten*
withstand	withstood	withstood	*widerstehen*
wring	wrung	wrung	*(aus-)wringen*
write	wrote	written	*schreiben*

grammar check – chapter by chapter

As you followed the exciting adventures of our heroes through the twenty-seven chapters, you will have noticed that each chapter had its own grammar points. The answers to the grammar tests appeared in the key with additional explanations. Below you will find a grammar check which tests the grammar points in more detail. The grammar check follows the chapters exactly. Find the answers on page 179. So we begin with:

Chapter 1

Past Perfect or Simple Past?

A. Blake and Heidi __________ (*leave*) the house before the Captain returned.

B. The Captain __________ (*throw*) Sam into the car. Then he __________ (*drive*) to Brighton.

C. After Jenny __________ (*go*), Bernd __________ (*notice*) that she had forgotten her handbag.

D. What you __________ (*do*) after you heard the police siren?

Chapter 2

Put in the Imperatives

A. __________ my questions immediately or you'll be very sorry about it.

a. *answer you* b. *answer*
c. *do answer* d. *answering*

B. (Geben Sie) __________ me the money now and we'll forget about the whole thing.

"__________ go to the cinema for a change, shall we?"

Chapter 3

Present Progressive or Present Simple?

A. Bernd: We're late for the cinema. What you __________ (*look*) for now?
Heidi: I can't find my purse.
Bernd: Why on earth you __________ (*not keep*) it in the same safe place all the time?

B. Jenny: You look very fit, Bernd. How often __________ jogging?
Bernd: I __________ to train every day.

a. *are you going* b. *do you go*
c. *try* d. *am trying*

C. Overheard in a pub:
"I'm the boss in my house alright. My wife never __________ (*tell*) me how to wash the dishes."

Chapter 4

Do you know your Statives (statische Verben)?

A. I __________ it's difficult for you, Heidi, but what __________ about the man who came into your room?

a. *know* b. *am knowing*
c. *do you remember* d. *are you remembering*

B. Sergeant: I __________ (*wollen*) an answer right now, or I'll arrest you on the spot.

C. Bernd: Heidi, how much money __________ Swindler? It must be a lot by now.

a. *do we owe* b. *are we owing*

Heidi: I don't know exactly but he often __________ stupid remarks about it.

c. *is making* d. *makes*

Chapter 5

A bit about Modals. Translate the German

A. We __________ (*könnten*) get into the house if we went through the backyard.

B. You __________ (*sollten*) certainly know who is working for the police force in Kent.

C. I __________ (*musste*) tie her up again or they would have known.

Fill in the blank:

D. "Do you serve women in this bar?"
"No, sir. You __________ bring your own."
a. *would* **b.** *must*

Chapter 6

Present Tenses again. Put in the Present Tenses

A. Why ______________ around in such a loud and aggressive way?
a. *are you always driving* **b.** *do you always drive*

B. Taxi driver: __________ (*Wollen Sie*) go to the cinema now or __________ (*bevorzugen Sie*) to go to a restaurant first?

C. Find the mistakes:
Jenny quite likes jogging but now she is owning a motorbike so she gets lazy.

D. _________________ that we'll have a change of government soon?
a. *do you think* **b.** *are you thinking*

Chapter 7

Put in the correct verb forms

Dear Debbie,

Thanks very much for your letter, which (1) __________ (*arrive*) more than six weeks ago! I (2) __________ (*mean*) to reply to it for ages, but I just (3) __________ (*not have*) time.

As you (4) __________ (*know*), I (5) __________ (*start*) a new job at the beginning of the month and I (6) __________ (*work*) incredibly hard ever since. It's quite interesting, and I (7) ___________ (*like*) my new boss, but I (8) __________ (*not finish*) until six o'clock and when I (9) __________ (*get*) home, I'm too tired to do anything! Anyway, I (10) __________ (*tell*) you all about it another time.

Yours Debbie

Chapter 8

Put into the Passive

A. Bernd, somebody wants you on the phone.

____

The police will interview you, for sure.

____

The policeman is asking her questions.

____

Put into the Active

B. Sorry, but in England your drinks must be paid for in advance.

____

You are expected by the German police to carry your I.D. (identity card) with you.

____

Chapter 9

A bit about Futures. Find the mistakes

A. When we arrive at the hotel Mr Swindler will sleep.
Let me take you home in the police car. I'll drive to Hastings anyway.

B. He: Darling, if we get married do you think you
_________ (be able) to live on my income?
She: Of course, darling, but what you _________ live on?

Chapter 10

Past Simple, Present Perfect again

A. Last week Blake _________ to sell the diamonds for £ 50,000.
a. *has managed* **b.** *managed*

_________ a man as dangerous as Sam?
a. *Have you ever met* **b.** *Did you ever meet*

B. **Find the mistakes:**
"How long have you stayed in Scotland?"
"I've been there for three years. Then I emigrated to Australia."

Chapter 11

Those Present Participles!

A. Rewrite the sentences using a Present Participle:

He welcomed Miss Mable and bowed politely to her.

____

He took no interest in us as he was interested in what was happening in the post office.

____

B. Replace the participles. Use a suitable conjunction:

Weather permitting, we'll go for a walk.

____

Walking through the park we had a bad argument.

____

C. Translate the German in the brackets:

I was teaching my girlfriend the tango when her father __________ (*kam hereingestürzt*). How was I to know he was stone deaf?

We all __________ (*standen da und warteten*) for the train in the pouring rain.

Chapter 12

More Tenses

A. What is the English for the German in the brackets?

What do you call a man who __________ (*verlieren*) half of his brain? A widower.

Nobody ever __________ (*sich beklagen*) about a parachute not opening.

B. Which is best? Simple or Progressive?

A man bought a parrot at an auction after some very brisk bidding. "I hope this bird talks," he said to the auctioneer.

"Does he talk? Who do you think __________ against you for the past twenty minutes?"

a. *has been bidding* **b.** *has bid*

She ____________ fifty of these anti-fat pills. Now she's so thin that every time she walks in the park, a dog tries to bury her.

a. *has taken* **b.** *has been taking*

Chapter 13

Passive – Active

A. The police sergeant's instructions. Put into the Passive:
Members of the public must sign the form.

____

You should pay your fines by five p.m.

____

Don't use recycled paper on photocopiers.

____

B. Build Passive sentences:
"Will you kiss me?"
"But I have scruples."
"That's okay. I ____________ (*be / vaccinate*)."

Bachelors know more about women than married men do.
If they didn't, they ________________ (*marry*) too.

C. Put the words in brackets into the Passive:
Advertising ____________ (*describe*) as the science of arresting the human intelligence long enough to get money from it.

Alcoholics Anonymous? Isn't it a place where whisky
____________ (*drink*) in secret?

Chapter 14

A bit about Adverbs and Adjectives

A. Spot the mistakes:
It was a serious accident and some people were bad injured.
Annette can run more far than me.

B. Which is correct?
When I take a long time, I'm __________ (*slowly / slow*).
When my boss takes a long time, he's ___________ (*thoroughly / thorough*).
People who cough __________ (*loudly / loud*) never go to the doctor. They go to the theatre or a concert.

Chapter 15

Real live Question Tags

A. Spot the mistakes:
You're going to give me the diamonds, or?
He can't have told us the truth, can't he?
There's a safe in your hotel, isn't it?

B. Put in the appropriate Question Tag:
Doctor: You're troubled with sexual fantasies, __________?
Patient: Oh no, doc. I rather enjoy them.

Chapter 16

More of those Adverbs and Adjectives

A. Which is correct?
That egg smells __________________ (*bad / badly*). You can't eat it.
Barbados is even __________________ (*beautifuller / more beautiful*) than Cuba.
The two authors worked ________________ (*hard / hardly*) for their publishing company, but it didn't help.

B. Put the words in brackets into the correct form.
Anne: I've just jogged twenty kilometres.
Ron: My God, that's the __________ (*far*) you've ever run.

Since he has been eating animal fat his arteries have become ____________ (*narrow*) and ____________ (*narrow*).

Chapter 17

It's all about Conditions

Fill in the correct form of the Conditional:

A. Security officer: Look, in this bottle there is a poisonous gas. Now, what steps ____________ (*you take*), if I dropped it?
Young scientist: Very large ones, sir!

B. Translate the German into English:
It is always the best policy to tell the truth, *vorausgesetzt, dass Sie ein ausgezeichneter Lügner sind.*

____

C. Put in the correct form of the Conditional:
More husbands would leave home if they ________________ (*know*) how to pack their suitcases.

Ron: What would you do in the case that you ____________ (*have*) rabies?
Bob: I ____________ (*ask*) for a pencil and a sheet of paper.
Ron: For your last will and testament?
Bob: No, to make a list of the people I ___________ (*bite*).

Chapter 18

A few more Conditions

A. Spot the mistakes:
If God would have wanted us to walk, he would never have given us the bicycle.
If I'd got drunk last night I would lose my driving licence.

B. Fill in the correct Conditionals:
Graffiti: If I had been the Virgin Mary I ____________ "No."
a. *had said* **b.** *would say* **c.** *would have said*

If Bernd had wanted to find Heidi, he ___________ into the house.
a. *should break* **b.** *should have broken* **c.** *had broken*

C. Build up the Conditionals:

Bernd: What would you have done if the Captain had arrived back early?

Blake: I ____________ (*leave*) through the window.

Jenny: Would you have explained the situation to Bernd if you ____________ (*meet*) him in the hotel room?

Heidi: I've no idea what I ____________ (*do*).

Chapter 19

What did they say?

A. What did Jenny say?

Direct Speech	Indirect Speech She said:
"I'm tired of all this overtime."	____________
"I was working in the accident ward	____________
when it happened."	____________
"I'll wait for Bernd in the restaurant."	____________

B. What were Bernd's actual words?

Bernd complained that he couldn't	____________
reserve a table.	____________
Bernd said he did two hours training	____________
every day.	____________
Bernd asked the policeman what sort of	____________
fine he would have to pay.	____________

Chapter 20

Gerund or Infinitive?

A. Spot the mistakes:

Clarity is the ability to give directions without to take your hands out of your pockets.

B. Gerund or Infinitive?

A man escaped from Hastings jail today by ____________ a wall. He had been sentenced for stealing diamonds.

a. *to climb* **b.** *climbing*

Chapter 21

Gerund or Infinitive?

A. Swindler: Well, sir, I hope you enjoyed ______________ (*staying/to stay*) with us.

Bernd: Yes, but I was rather hoping ______________ (*to stay/staying*) much longer since I've practically bought the place.

Wyatt Earp: It's lonely __________ (*to be/being*) in the saddle now that the horse is dead.

B. Spot the mistakes:

I don't mind being average because it means I'm as close to the top as I am to the bottom.

Swindler: I gave my wife a lecture on economising as you told me.
Mable: Any result?
Swindler: Yes, I had to give up to smoke.

Third world aid means to transfer money from the rich countries to the rich in poor countries.

Chapter 22

Mix up those ___ings!

A. Spot the mistakes:

When in Paris, I always eat at Eiffel Tower restaurant because it's the only place where I can avoid seeing the damned thing.

B. Put in the correct forms:

__________ is something you should not do if you don't want soot in your lungs.

a. *to smoke* b. *smoking* c. *having smoked*

I really hate __________. It gives me back-ache.

a. *ironing* b. *to iron*

C. "Used to" or "be used to ___ing"?

I __________ a werewolf, but I'm alright noooooooooow!

a. *used to be* b. *am used to being*

Chapter 23

A. Spot the mistakes:
Bob is certainly much thinner as he was two years ago.
I studied at college. Than I enrolled in a course at university.
As more I try, as more I make mistakes.

B. Put in the correct forms of some and any:
I'm sorry. I don't know ______ way I can get this engine to start.
Does ______ here know how I can get to the main railway station?
I have ______ free evenings this week. Shall we do a bit of training together?

Chapter 24

A. Which is best?
When you read this picture postcard ______________________
a. *I'll be lying on the beach in Barbados.*
b. *I'm going to lie on the beach in Barbados.*

When we get home ____________________________________
a. *I'll be going to bed immediately.*
b. *I'll go to bed immediately.*

B. Spot the mistake with the adverbs:
Okay, I'll come to the point straight. We have to fire him.

It must have been more easy to pass your motor-bike test in your day. I've failed it three times.

Chapter 25

A. The following are headlines. Find the correct participle of the verb in the brackets:

Pilot tells of ____________ (*amaze*) escape.
Football star in hospital with ___________ (*break*) leg.
Police search for ____________ (*miss*) child.
____________ (*worry*) German searches for his girlfriend.

B. Build sentences with participles:
You spent the night in a house where strange things happened. Use the ideas below to make sentences about what you SAW, HEARD and FELT.

Example:
Someone screamed → I heard someone scream.
A figure was dancing ... → I saw a figure dancing ...

Someone was crying in the next room.

____

A cold hand touched me.

____

A white face appeared and then disappeared.

____

Someone tapped me on the shoulder.

____

Chapter 26

Preposition workshop

A. A member of Parliament is talking to his secretary. Put in the prepositions.

M.P. Right, Simon, what's the programme?

Simon: Rather busy, I'm afraid, sir. There's a meeting tomorrow (1) ________ nine o'clock, which will probably go on (2) ________ lunchtime. Then (3) ________ lunch you've got an appointment with the Prime Minister. She's expecting you (4) ________ 2.15 and 2.30. Incidentally, the Foreign Secretary would like a word with you sometime (5) ________ the afternoon.

M.P. The Foreign Secretary? But I thought he was flying to Paris (6) ________ the morning.

Simon: He was, sir, but that visit's been cancelled because of the French elections. He's now going (7) ________ July instead, but no one knows exactly when.

M.P. Oh, I see. What else?

Simon: Well, (8) ________ Thursday you've got another meeting, which is scheduled to last (9) ________ 10.00 a.m. (10) ________ 12.00 p.m. Oh, and I almost forgot, the Home Secretary wants to see you (11) ________ the meeting starts. He said it wouldn't take long.

M.P. I wonder what he wants.

key to grammar check

Chapter 1

A. had left
B. threw, drove
C. had gone, noticed
D. did you do

Chapter 2

A. **b.** answer
B. Give me
C. Let's

Chapter 3

A. are you looking, don't you keep
B. **b.** do you go, c. try
C. tells

Chapter 4

A. **a.** know c. do you remember
B. want
C. **a.** do we owe, **d.** makes

Chapter 5

A. could
B. should/ought to
C. had to
D. **b.** must

Chapter 6

A. **b.** Do you always drive
B. Do you want to, do you prefer / would you prefer

C. now she owns, so she is getting

D. **a.** Do you think

Chapter 7

1. arrived
2. have (I've) been meaning
3. haven't had
4. know
5. started
6. have (I've) been working
7. like
8. don't finish
9. get
10. will (I'll) tell

Chapter 8

A. Bernd, you are wanted on the phone.
You will be interviewed by the police for sure.
She is being asked questions by the policeman.

B. Sorry, but in England you must pay for your drinks in advance.
The German police expect you to carry your I.D. with you.

Chapter 9

A. ... Mr. Swindler will be sleeping.
I'll be driving to Hastings anyway.

B. ... you will be able to live ...
but what are you going to live on.

Chapter 10

A. **b.** managed
a. Have you ever met

B. How long did you stay ...
I was there for three years.

Chapter 11

A. He welcomed Miss Mable bowing politely to her.
He took no interest in us only being interested in what was happening in the post-office.

B. If the weather is okay, we'll go for a walk.
When we were walking through the park ...

C. came running in
stood waiting

Chapter 12

A. has lost
has ever complained

B. **a.** has been bidding
a. has taken

Chapter 13

A. The form must be signed by members of the public.
Your fines should be paid by five p.m.
Recycled paper must not be used on photocopiers.

B. ... I have been vaccinated.
they would be married too.

C. is described
is drunk

Chapter 14

A. ... were badly injured
run farther / further than me.

B. ... I'm slow
he's thorough
loudly

Chapter 15

A ..., aren't you ?
..., can he?
..., isn't there?

B. ..., aren't you?

Chapter 16

A. bad
more beautiful than
hard

B. the furthest / farthest
narrower and narrower

Chapter 17

A. would you take
B. provided that you are an excellent liar.
C. knew
had, would ask, would bite

Chapter 18

A. If God had wanted us ...
... I would have lost my driving licence.
B. c. would have said
b. should have broken
C. I would have left through the window.
... if you had met him, ... what I would have done

Chapter 19

A. She said she was tired of all that overtime.
She said she had been working in the accident ward when it happened.
She said she would wait for Bernd in the restaurant.

B. "I can't reserve a table."
"I do two hours training every day."
"What sort of fine will I have to pay?"

Chapter 20

A. Clarity is the ability to give directions without taking your hands out of your pockets.
B. climbing

Chapter 21

A. ... enjoyed staying, ... hoping to stay
... being
B. no mistake
... give up smoking
... means transferring

Chapter 22

A. no mistake

B. **b.** Smoking

a. ironing

C. **a.** I used to be ...

Chapter 23

A. ... thinner than ...

Then I enrolled ...

The more I try, the more I make mistakes.

B. any way

anybody / anyone

some

Chapter 24

A. **a.** I'll be lying

b. I'll go to bed

B. Okay, I'll come straight to the point.

It must have been easier to ...

Chapter 25

A. amazing

broken

missing

worried

B. I heard someone crying.

I felt a cold hand touch / touching me.

I saw a white face appear and then disappear.

I felt someone tap me on the shoulder.

Chapter 26

A. (1) at
(2) until/till
(3) after
(4) between
(5) in / during
(6) in
(7) in
(8) on
(9) from
(10) to / till
(11) before

a

abandon ship	*das sinkende Schiff verlassen*
abduction	*Entführung*
able; be ~ to	*können, in der Lage sein zu*
about; cost ~ 60 pounds	*ungefähr 60 Pfund kosten*
abroad; go ~	*ins Ausland gehen*
accelerator	*Gaspedal*
accept	*akzeptieren; aufnehmen*
access to the Internet	*Internetzugang*
accident report	*Unfallbericht*
accident ward	*Unfallstation*
accident; have an ~	*einen Unfall haben*
accidents happen	*Unfälle passieren*
accommodation	*Unterkunft*
accompany	*begleiten*
according to this	*demnach*
account	*Konto*
ache	*schmerzen; Schmerz*
achievement	*Leistung*
acquaintance	*Bekannte(r)*
acquainted; be ~ with	*bekannt sein mit, kennen*
action; take ~	*etwas unternehmen, zur Tat schreiten*
actually	*eigentlich, tatsächlich*
actually take place	*tatsächlich stattfinden*
adventure	*Abenteuer*
advert	*Annonce*
after all	*immerhin, schließlich*
age	*Alter*
agree with someone on something	*sich mit jemandem über etwas einigen*
aim; ~ at	*Ziel; zielen auf*

ajar; the door stood ~	*die Tür war angelehnt*
alive and kicking	*quicklebendig*
allow someone to do something	*jemandem erlauben etwas zu tun*
allowed; be ~ to	*dürfen*
all's well that ends well	*Ende gut, alles gut*
almost	*fast*
already	*schon*
although	*obwohl*
altogether	*alles zusammen*
amazed	*verblüfft*
ambulance	*Krankenwagen*
ambulance man	*Sanitäter*
animal	*Tier*
anti-fat pills	*Schlankheitspillen*
anxious days	*bange Tage*
anyway	*dennoch*
apologise to someone for something	*sich bei jemandem für etwas entschuldigen*
apology	*Entschuldigung*
apparently	*offensichtlich, anscheinend*
appear; it doesn't ~ to be what it seems	*scheinen, erscheinen; auftauchen; es ist nicht so, wie es scheint*
application	*Bewerbung; Anwendung*
appointment; make an ~	*Verabredung, Termin; sich verabreden*
approach someone	*sich jemandem nähern*
argument; have an ~	*Streit haben*
arm of the sofa	*Sofalehne*
around	*umher, herum*
arrange a date	*einen Termin vereinbaren*
arrive in England	*in England ankommen*
art; the ~ of saying nothing	*die Kunst nichts zu sagen*
as	*wie; als; da*
ashtray	*Aschenbecher*
assemble	*zusammenbauen; sich versammeln*
assemble a car	*ein Auto zusammenbauen*
assist someone	*jemandem helfen*
assistance; how can I be of ~?	*was kann ich für Sie tun?*

assortment	*Sortiment*
astonishment	*Erstaunen*
at least; for ~ ~ a week	*wenigstens, mindestens eine Woche*
at this time	*um diese Zeit*
attention, please!	*Achtung, bitte!*
attentively; listen~	*aufmerksam zuhören*
attracted; feel ~ to someone	*sich zu jemandem hingezogen fühlen*
aunt	*Tante*
available; I'm ~ at any time	*ich stehe jederzeit zur Verfügung*
aware; I'm ~ of it	*mir ist es klar; ich bin mir dessen bewusst*

b

back in Germany	*daheim / zurück in Deutschland*
back; the ~ of a building	*die Rückseite eines Gebäudes*
background	*Hintergrund*
bacon	*Speck*
bag	*Beutel*
baggage; get rid of unwanted ~	*unerwünschten Ballast loswerden*
bang on the door	*gegen die Tür hämmern*
bargain	*ein gutes Geschäft; Schnäppchen*
barge in on	*hereinplatzen*
basement	*Keller*
battle	*Schlacht*
be lucky	*Glück haben*
be in time	*rechtzeitig kommen*
beach	*Strand*
bean	*Bohne*
bear heavily on	*schwer lasten ... auf*
bear on; bring one's enquiring mind to ~ ~ the problem	*seine Neugier dem Problem zuwenden*
bear, have one's own cross to ~	*sein eigenes Kreuz zu tragen haben*
bear (bore, born); be born	*geboren sein*
bearer; signature of ~	*Unterschrift des Inhabers*
become rich	*reich werden*
bedroom	*Schlafzimmer*
bed-sheet	*Bettlaken*
beggar	*Bettler*

beggars can't be choosers	*keine andere Wahl haben*
begin, began, begun	*anfangen, beginnen*
believe something	*etwas glauben*
belong to somebody else	*jemand anderem gehören*
bench	*(Park-)Bank*
bend over him	*sich beugen über*
bet	*wetten*
beyond	*jenseits*
bicycle	*Fahrrad*
bill; put it on my ~	*schreiben Sie es auf meine Rechnung*
block of concrete	*Betonklotz*
blood pressure	*Blutdruck*
blood sample	*Blutprobe*
blow; till all this has blown over	*bis Gras darüber gewachsen ist*
board	*Tafel*
bogus; a ~ inspector	*ein falscher Inspektor*
bold(ly)	*kühn*
bolt	*Bolzen*
bonnet	*Kühlerhaube*
book a room	*ein Zimmer reservieren*
booked; be ~ in	*eine Reservierung haben*
boring	*langweilig*
born in London	*in London geboren*
borrow something	*sich etwas leihen*
bother someone	*jemanden belästigen*
bottom	*Boden, Grund*
bottom left-hand corner	*linke untere Ecke*
brain	*Gehirn*
brainwave	*guter Einfall*
brake; hit the ~	*auf die Bremse treten*
brand new	*nagelneu*
break a journey	*eine Reise unterbrechen*
break into (broke, broken)	*einbrechen in*
break into a run	*losrennen*
break off	*abbrechen*
breast of duck	*Entenbrust*
breath	*Atem*

breathe	*atmen; hauchen*
bred; be ~ in the docklands	*im Hafenviertel aufwachsen*
briefcase	*Aktenkoffer*
bright red hair	*leuchtend rote Haare*
bring forward plans	*Pläne beschleunigen/vorziehen*
bring someone into one's plans	*jemanden in seine Pläne einweihen*
brochure; look at a ~	*eine Broschüre anschauen*
broom cupboard	*Besenkammer*
brown bags	*Papiertüten*
build, built, built	*bauen*
bulb	*(Glüh-)Birne*
bundle someone up	*jemanden verschnüren*
bundle someone into...	*jemand verfrachten, wegpacken*
bury	*be-, vergraben*
business; it's not my ~	*Geschäft; es geht mich nichts an*
buy, bought, bought	*kaufen*
by any chance	*zufällig*
by now	*bis jetzt, inzwischen*
by the way	*übrigens*

C

call a hotel	*ein Hotel anrufen*
call round	*vorbeischauen*
caller	*Anrufer*
calm down	*sich beruhigen*
cancer	*Krebs (Krankheit)*
candle	*Kerze*
car rental company	*Mietwagenfirma*
car wash	*Autowaschanlage*
car-chase	*Verfolgungsjagd im Auto*
care; I don't ~ if ...	*es ist mir egal, wenn ...*
carefully	*vorsichtig*
carpet	*Teppich*
carriage	*Waggon*
carrier	*Träger; Tragebehälter*
case; a ~ in question	*ein typischer Fall*
case; in any ~	*jedenfalls*

cash	*Bargeld*
cash dispenser	*Geldautomat*
casually; look ~ around	*lässig umherblicken*
catch (caught, caught) on a nail	*an einem Nagel hängen bleiben*
catch up with someone	*jemanden einholen*
catch; the ~ of a bag	*der Verschluss einer Tasche*
cause trouble	*Probleme / Ärger verursachen*
cellar	*Keller*
centigrade	*Grad Celsius*
century	*Jahrhundert*
certain(ly)	*gewiss, sicher(lich)*
chamber maid	*Zimmermädchen*
chance; take no ~	*kein Risiko eingehen*
change	*umsteigen, wechseln*
change gear	*in einen anderen Gang schalten*
change into	*verwandeln, wechseln*
changing cubicle	*Umkleidekabine*
channel	*Programm*
chase	*Jagd; jagen*
cheap; get it ~	*es billig bekommen*
cheeky	*frech*
choice; have no ~	*Auswahl; Wahl; keine andere Wahl haben*
choose (chose, chosen)	*wählen*
circumstances	*Umstände*
clay pipe	*Tonpfeife*
clean a room	*ein Zimmer sauber machen*
clear up	*Klarschiff machen*
closer; come a little ~	*etwas näher kommen*
cloth bag	*Stoffsack*
clue	*Hinweis*
clue; have a ~	*einen Hinweis, Ahnung haben*
clutch	*Kupplung*
coast; the ~ is clear	*die Luft ist rein*
collapse	*zusammenbrechen*
collide with	*zusammenstoßen mit*
come across as an eternity	*wie eine Ewigkeit erscheinen*

come across the motive for this crime	*auf das Motiv des Verbrechens stoßen*
come into some money	*zu Geld kommen*
come on!	*komm schon!*
come round	*zu Bewusstsein kommen*
comfortable; make someone ~	*es jemandem bequem machen*
commercial line	*Firmenanschluss (Telefon)*
compare prices	*Preise vergleichen*
compartment	*Abteil*
complain about	*sich beschweren über, reklamieren*
concrete	*Beton*
concussion	*Gehirnerschütterung*
condemn	*verurteilen*
condition of life	*Lebensumstand/Lebenssituation*
confidence	*Zuversicht, Vertrauen*
confirm	*bestätigen*
confirmation	*Bestätigung*
confuse someone	*jemanden verwirren*
connected with; be ~	*verbunden werden mit*
connection	*Anschlusszug; Verbindung*
conscience	*Gewissen*
constable	*Wachtmeister*
constabulary	*Polizei(-truppe)*
consultant	*Berater*
contact / telephone someone	*jemanden anrufen*
contact someone	*sich in Verbindung setzen mit*
contact someone	*jemanden erreichen / sprechen*
convert	*umrüsten, verwandeln*
convert into euros	*in Euros umrechnen*
cook	*Koch; kochen*
copper, cop (slang)	*Polizist, Bulle*
corner	*Ecke*
corner; table in the ~	*ein Tisch in der Ecke*
cosiness	*Gemütlichkeit*
cosy; a ~ fire	*ein gemütliches Kaminfeuer*
counter	*Schalter*
country hotel	*Landgasthof*

county	*Grafschaft*
couple; a ~ of things	*ein paar Dinge*
couple; a loving ~	*ein liebendes Paar*
couple; a married ~	*Paar; Ehepaar*
course	*Kurs; Gericht, Gang (Speise)*
course; during the ~ of three days	*im Verlauf von drei Tagen*
course; of ~	*natürlich*
cracking; let's get ~!	*auf geht's!*
crackle	*prasseln, knistern*
craftsman	*Handwerksmeister*
crash into a tree	*gegen einen Baum fahren*
cream tea	*Engl. Spezialität: Tee mit Rosinenbrötchen, Erdbeerkonfitüre und Schlagsahne*
create Heaven and Earth	*Himmel und Erde erschaffen*
criminal	*Verbrecher*
cross the Channel	*den Kanal überqueren*
cuisine	*die gute Küche*
curb	*Randstein*
customer	*Kunde*
customise	*nach Maß fertigen*
cut a rope	*ein Seil durchschneiden*
cut; ~ a long story short	*kurz gesagt*

d

damaged; badly ~	*schwer beschädigt*
damp cloth	*feuchtes Tuch*
dangerous	*gefährlich*
dare	*wagen*
dare; how ~ you?	*wie können Sie es wagen?*
darken; his face darkened	*sein Gesicht verfinsterte sich*
dashboard	*Armaturenbrett*
date	*Datum, Rendezvous*
date; get a ~ with	*ein Rendezvous bekommen mit*
deal with	*sich kümmern um; erledigen*
deal with people	*mit Leuten zu tun haben*
decide to do	*sich entschließen, etwas zu tun*

deep-fried breaded Brie	*frittierter Briekäse*
defect	*Fehler*
degree centigrade	*Grad Celsius*
delay	*Verspätung; aufhalten*
deliver goods	*Waren (ab-)liefern*
depart	*abfahren*
departure	*Abfahrt*
departure times	*Abfahrzeiten*
deposit; pay a ~	*eine Anzahlung machen*
describe someone	*jemanden beschreiben*
dessert	*Nachtisch*
destination; fix a ~	*ein Ziel festlegen*
detail	*Einzelheit*
devil ; What the ~ ...	*Was zum Teufel ...*
dial the wrong number	*die falsche Nummer wählen*
die	*sterben*
die down; the fire dies ~	*das Feuer verlischt*
difference; it makes no ~	*es macht keinen Unterschied*
different from	*anders als, verschieden*
difficult to use	*schwierig zu handhaben*
difficulty	*Schwierigkeit*
direct line to heaven	*direkter Draht zum Himmel*
dirt	*Dreck*
disappear	*verschwinden*
disappointed	*enttäuscht*
disaster	*Katastrophe*
disastrous	*verheerend*
discount	*Rabatt*
discourage someone	*jemanden entmutigen*
disease	*Krankheit*
dishes; do the ~	*Geschirr spülen*
dislocate one's shoulder	*seine Schulter ausrenken*
disused quarry	*stillgelegter Steinbruch*
do someone in	*jemanden kalt machen*
docklands	*Hafenviertel*
doorframe	*Türrahmen*
double (room)	*Doppelzimmer*

double the price	*den Preis verdoppeln*
downside	*das Schlechte, Kehrseite*
draughty	*zugig*
dreadful	*fürchterlich*
dream about / of	*träumen von*
dressed elegantly	*elegant gekleidet*
drift; ~ into a room	*schlendern; sich treiben lassen; in einen Raum schlendern*
drive into a tree	*gegen einen Baum fahren*
driver	*Fahrer*
driving licence	*Führerschein*
drop	*Tropfen*
drop in at	*vorbeischauen bei*
drop into	*reinschauen*
drop into first gear	*in den ersten Gang herunterschalten*
drop someone off	*jemanden absetzen, aussteigen lassen*
drop something	*etwas fallen lassen*
drug	*Medikament, Droge*
drug someone	*jemanden betäuben*
drunk	*betrunken*
dumbo	*Trottel*
dusk	*Abenddämmerung*
duty; be on ~	*Dienst haben*
dye; ~ one's hair	*färben; sich die Haare färben*

e

eager	*eifrig, begierig*
eagerly; await someone ~	*jemand sehnlich erwarten*
eagle	*Adler*
early, earlier	*früh, früher*
early; half an hour ~	*eine halbe Stunde zu früh*
early; the ~ hours	*die frühen Stunden*
earn money	*Geld verdienen*
ears; I'm all ~	*ich bin ganz Ohr*
easy	*leicht*
edgeways; be unable to get a word in ~	*nicht zu Wort kommen*

education	*Ausbildung; Erziehung*
efficient	*tüchtig*
eight years ago	*vor acht Jahren*
else; someone ~	*jemand anderes*
emergency	*Notfall*
emergency service	*Pannenhilfe*
emperor	*Kaiser*
employ people	*Leute einstellen*
empress	*Kaiserin*
empty a bottle	*eine Flasche (ent-)leeren*
empty houses	*leere Häuser*
empty promises	*leere Versprechen*
enemy	*Feind*
engaged to someone	*verlobt mit jemandem*
engine	*Motor*
enjoy	*genießen*
enjoy your stay!	*angenehmen Aufenthalt!*
enjoy; did you ~ your meal?	*hat es Ihnen geschmeckt?*
enter the pin number	*die Pinnummer eingeben*
enterprising	*unternehmungslustig*
entertaining; are you ~ ?	*haben Sie Gäste?*
error	*Irrtum, Fehler*
escape	*Flucht; fliehen; entkommen*
escort	*begleiten; Begleitung*
especially	*besonders*
eternity; come across as an ~	*wie eine Ewigkeit erscheinen*
even	*sogar*
even darker	*sogar noch dunkler*
events	*Ereignisse*
eventually	*schließlich*
every second day	*jeder zweite Tag*
every Tom, Dick and Harry	*Hinz und Kunz*
everything in good time	*alles zu seiner Zeit*
evidence; give evidence	*aussagen*
evil-looking	*finster aussehend*
except	*außer*
exchange words	*Worte austauschen*

expect something	*etwas erwarten*
expensive	*teuer*
experience	*Erlebnis; Erfahrung*
experience; a bad ~	*ein schlimmes Erlebnis*
explain something to someone	*jemandem etwas erklären*
extract of an article	*Auszug aus einem Artikel*
face	*Gesicht*
facilities	*Einrichtungen*
fail; ~ to do something	*misslingen; versagen; versäumen, etwas zu tun*
fall off; (fell, fallen)	*herunterfallen*
famous; a ~ novelist	*eine berühmte Romanautorin*
famous; world ~	*weltberühmt*
fancy clothes	*schicke Kleider*
fancy someone	*jemanden mögen*
fast-thinking Blake	*der Schnelldenker Blake*
fault; it's your ~	*es ist deine Schuld*
favourite; his ~ drink	*sein Lieblingsgetränk*
fear	*Furcht; befürchten*
feel safer (felt, felt)	*sich sicherer fühlen*
feel sick	*einem schlecht sein*
feet; get cold ~	*kalte Füße bekommen*
female	*weiblich*
fence	*Zaun*
fetch the suitcase	*den Koffer holen*
few; a ~	*wenige; ein paar*
fiancée / fiancé	*Verlobte(r)*
fickle	*sprunghaft*
file something	*etwas zu den Akten legen*
fill her up, please	*voll tanken, bitte*
fill out a form	*ein Formular ausfüllen*
fine; I'm ~	*mir geht's gut*
fingerprint	*Fingerabdruck*
fireplace	*Kamin*
fireside atmosphere	*Kaminfeueratmosphäre*

first thing in the morning	*gleich morgen früh*
fishy; a ~ character	*ein zwielichtiger / verdächtiger Mensch*
fit of conscience	*Gewissensbiss*
fit perfectly	*perfekt passen, sitzen*
flash of lightning	*Blitz*
flashing light	*hier: Blaulicht*
flashy	*protzig*
flat share	*Wohngemeinschaft*
flight	*Flug*
floor	*Boden*
fly	*Fliege*
flying foreigner	*fliegender Ausländer*
folder	*Mappe*
for short	*abgekürzt*
force someone to do something	*jemanden zwingen, etwas zu tun*
forehead	*Stirn*
foreign; a ~ country	*ein fremdes Land*
foreigner	*Ausländer*
forget to pay (forgot, forgotten)	*vergessen zu zahlen*
fork	*Gabel*
form	*Formular*
fortunately	*zum Glück*
forward(s)	*vorwärts*
forwarding address	*Nachsendeadresse*
free someone	*jemanden befreien*
freeze, froze, frozen	*erstarren; einfrieren*
freshen up	*sich frisch machen*
fridge	*Eisschrank*
front page	*erste Seite*
fumble for the key	*nach dem Schlüssel fummeln*
fumble with	*herumfummeln an / mit*
further away	*weiter weg*
further clues	*weitere Hinweise*

gadget	*Spielerei*
gain time	*Zeit gewinnen*
gardener	*Gärtner*
gaze at	*starren auf*
gear; change into first ~	*in den ersten Gang schalten*
gender	*Geschlecht*
gentlemanly	*vornehm, fein*
get a move on	*sich beeilen*
get away with	*davonkommen*
get into an affair	*sich auf eine Affäre einlassen*
get over the flu	*eine Grippe auskurieren*
get rid of something	*etwas loswerden*
get the picture	*klar sehen; verstehen*
get through to someone	*jemanden telefonisch erreichen*
get used to something	*sich an etwas gewöhnen*
giggle	*kichern*
give directions	*Anweisungen geben*
give one's opinion	*seine Meinung sagen*
give someone away	*jemanden verraten*
glad; I'm ~	*ich bin froh*
glasses	*Brille*
glove	*Handschuh*
glum	*bedrückt*
go abroad	*ins Ausland gehen*
go into hiding	*untertauchen*
go upstairs / downstairs	*hinauf- / hinuntergehen*
go wrong	*schief gehen*
gone; be ~	*verschwunden; verschwinden*
goody	*eine tolle Sache, ein tolles Ding*
goose pimples	*Gänsehaut*
governor (slang)	*Chef*
grab something	*etwas packen, ergreifen*
grate	*Kaminrost*
grateful	*dankbar*
groan	*stöhnen*
grubby	*schmutzig*
grumble	*murren*

guard; be off one's ~	*unachtsam sein*
guardian of law and order	*Hüter von Recht und Ordnung*
guess; I ~	*raten; annehmen; ich vermute*
guest	*Gast*
guilty	*schuldig*
gulp (of whisky)	*Schluck (Whisky)*
guy	*Typ, Kerl*

h

habit-forming; be ~	*süchtig machen*
hair-raising adventures	*haarsträubende Abenteuer*
half board	*Halbpension*
half past ten	*halb elf*
halt	*Stillstand*
handbrake	*Handbremse*
handsome	*fesch, gutaussehend*
happen quickly	*schnell passieren*
happen; accidents ~	*Unfälle passieren*
hardly	*kaum*
hatch a plan	*einen Plan ausbrüten*
headache; have a ~	*Kopfweh haben*
health and hygiene authorities	*Gesundheitsamt*
hear movements (heard, heard)	*Schritte hören*
heart; he felt his ~ sink	*das Herz fiel ihm in die Hosentasche*
heat a room	*ein Zimmer (be-)heizen*
heaven	*Himmel*
heels; high ~	*hohe Absätze*
height	*Größe, Höhe*
height; stand up to one's full ~	*sich zu seiner vollen Größe aufrichten*
help someone further	*jemandem weiterhelfen*
here you are	*bitte sehr*
hero, pl. heroes	*Held, Helden*
hesitate	*zögern*
hide	*(Tier-)Haut, Fell*
hide (hid, hidden)	*(sich) verstecken*
highly motivated	*hoch motiviert*
hiss between one's teeth	*durch die Zähne zischen*

hit the brake (hit, hit)	*auf die Bremse treten*
hit; the shot ~ the mirror	*der Schuss traf den Spiegel*
hoist up	*hochhieven*
hold on a minute!	*Moment mal!*
hold; get ~ of	*etwas bekommen; erlangen*
honour	*Ehre*
horrible	*schrecklich*
host; hostess	*Gastgeber(in)*
hostage	*Geisel*
hour; run on the ~	*zu jeder jede vollen Stunde fahren*
how come that...?	*wie kommt es, dass ...?*
huge	*riesig*
human being	*menschliches Wesen*
humid	*feucht; schwül*
hurry	*Eile; sich beeilen*
hurry up!	*beeil dich!*
hurt somebody (hurt, hurt)	*jemandem wehtun*
husband	*Ehemann*

i

identity card	*Ausweis*
ignition	*Zündung*
illuminating	*aufschlussreich*
imagine something	*sich etwas vorstellen*
immediately	*sofort, umgehend*
impatient	*ungeduldig*
impossible	*unmöglich*
in a flash	*blitzschnell*
in any case	*auf alle Fälle*
in fact	*in der Tat*
in front of the car	*vor dem Auto*
incompetent	*unfähig*
indeed	*wirklich, tatsächlich*
indeed; yes ~	*ja, das stimmt; in der Tat*
indicate	*hindeuten auf*
indisposed; be ~	*unpässlich sein*
influence	*Einfluss*

injured persons	*verletzte Personen*
innocent	*unschuldig*
insist; if you ~	*wenn Sie darauf bestehen*
inspect	*untersuchen*
install a kitchen	*eine Küche einbauen*
instead of	*anstatt*
insure oneself against ...	*sich gegen ... versichern*
intention	*Absicht*
internal bleeding	*innere Blutungen*
interrupt someone	*jemanden unterbrechen*
interview room	*Verhörzimmer*
intrigued; be ~	*neugierig sein*
invent	*erfinden*
invite someone	*jemanden einladen*
invoice	*Rechnung*
involved; be ~ in a crime	*in ein Verbrechen verwickelt sein*
issue	*Angelegenheit; Frage, Sache*
issue; get to the bottom of an ~	*einer Sache auf den Grund gehen*
item	*Punkt*

j

join someone	*sich jemandem anschließen; sich gesellen zu*
joint; put a shoulder back in ~	*Gelenk; eine Schulter wieder einrenken*
journey; go on a ~	*eine Reise machen*
just about everything	*so ziemlich alles*
just arrived from ...	*gerade aus ... angekommen*
just in time	*gerade rechtzeitig*

k

keen; be ~ on	*große Lust haben zu ...*
keep talking	*weiterreden*
key	*Taste*
key; give me the ~	*gib mir die Schlüssel*
kitchen	*Küche*
knock at the door	*anklopfen*
knock on the head	*auf den Kopf hauen*

knock someone down/over	*jemanden überfahren*
know (knew, known)	*wissen, kennen*
knowing; a ~ smile	*ein wissendes Lächeln*
knowledge	*Wissen*
knowledge of this world	*Lebenserfahrung*
lamb	*Lamm*
lane; a country ~	*schmale Landstraße*
last five minutes	*fünf Minuten dauern*
last for ever	*ewig dauern*
late afternoon	*später Nachmittag*
lawyer; speak to a ~	*einen Anwalt sprechen*
lean back	*sich zurücklehnen*
leatherwear	*Lederwaren*
leave a message (left, left)	*eine Nachricht hinterlassen*
leave me alone	*lass mich in Ruhe*
leave (left, left)	*verlassen*
leave, ~ a door open	*eine Tür offen lassen*
left; have one car ~	*ein Auto übrig haben*
left-hand drive	*Linkssteuerung*
let someone down	*jemanden im Stich lassen*
lie down	*sich hinlegen*
lie; tell lies	*lügen; Lügen erzählen*
lift the phone	*den Hörer abnehmen*
light	*Licht*
lightning; like a flash of ~	*wie der Blitz*
lights flashing and the siren howling	*mit Blaulicht und Sirene*
limited to	*beschränkt auf*
liquid	*Flüssigkeit*
listen to someone	*jemandem zuhören*
living room	*Wohnzimmer*
local	*aus dem Ort, ortsansässig*
local; the ~ police station	*das örtliche Polizeirevier*
located; be ~ between two houses	*sich zwischen zwei Häusern befinden*
lock the door	*die Tür abschließen*

log	*Holzscheit*
long; be ~	*spät kommen; auf sich warten lassen*
look each other over	*sich gegenseitig mustern*
look out across	*Blick / Aussicht haben über*
look what the cat's dragged in	*sieh da, wen haben wir denn da*
lose money	*Geld verlieren*
lose (lost, lost)	*verlieren*
loss	*Verlust*
lost your way?	*ihr habt euch wohl verlaufen*
lots of bookings	*viele Buchungen*
lounge	*Aufenthaltsraum*
lovely; a ~ hotel	*ein reizendes Hotel*
low table	*Couchtisch*
Ltd (Limited)	*GmbH*
lukewarm	*lauwarm*
lunatic asylum	*Irrenhaus*

m

magnifying glass	*Lupe*
main course	*Hauptgericht*
make a booking	*etwas buchen*
make mistakes	*Fehler machen*
make up for	*wieder gutmachen*
male	*männlich*
malicious damage	*vorsätzliche Beschädigung*
manage okay	*zurechtkommen*
manage; be able to ~ with something	*mit etwas umgehen können*
mansion	*Herrenhaus*
map	*Straßenkarte*
map; spread a ~ out	*eine Landkarte ausbreiten*
married	*verheiratet*
match something	*zu etwas passen*
matter	*Sache*
mean	*bedeuten*
mean; he's so ~	*er ist so geizig*
meanwhile	*inzwischen*

mechanic	*Mechaniker*
medication; take ~	*Medikamente nehmen*
meet, met, met	*treffen, begegnen*
mention something	*etwas erwähnen*
menu	*Speisekarte*
mess; leave the room in a ~	*das Zimmer als Saustall hinterlassen*
middle; in the ~ of the night	*mitten in der Nacht*
might; you ~ have been killed	*du hättest getötet werden können*
milometer	*Kilometerzähler*
mind; be on someone's ~	*jemanden (geistig) beschäftigen*
mink coat	*Nerzmantel*
mirror	*Spiegel*
misfortune	*Unglück, Pech*
miss	*vermissen; verpassen*
miss someone	*jemanden vermissen*
mistake; by ~	*aus Versehen*
misunderstand	*missverstehen*
mix-up	*Verwechslung*
mobile (phone)	*Handy*
moreover	*darüber hinaus*
motorway	*Autobahn*
move; on the ~	*unterwegs*
movement	*Bewegung*
mud	*Matsch*
muddy road	*matschige Straße*
muff out a candle	*eine Kerze ausdrücken*
mumble in German	*auf Deutsch murmeln*
mutter something	*etwas murmeln*
mysterious	*geheimnisvoll*

n

nail	*Nagel*
name; reserve in the ~ of	*auf den Namen von ... reservieren*
narrow country road	*enge Landstraße*
nasty; be a ~ piece of work	*fies; ein fieser Kerl sein*
nature reserve	*Naturschutzgebiet*

navigator	*Lotse*
near to the beach	*in der Nähe des Strands*
near to the reception	*nahe der Rezeption*
nearest; the ~ telephone box	*das nächstgelegene Telefon*
necessary	*notwendig*
need to do	*tun müssen*
needs	*Bedürfnisse*
neighbour	*Nachbar*
nephew	*Neffe*
nevertheless	*dennoch*
night and day	*Tag und Nacht*
nightcap	*Gutenachttrunk*
noise	*Geräusch, Lärm*
not at all	*überhaupt nicht*
not know which way to turn (knew, known)	*nicht wissen, was man machen soll*
nothing at all	*überhaupt nichts*
notice something	*etwas bemerken*
notion; have you any ~ of ...?	*haben Sie eine Vorstellung von ...?*
now and again	*hin und wieder*
nowadays	*heutzutage*
nurse	*Krankenschwester*

O

obviously	*offensichtlich*
odd; the ~ couple	*das ungleiche Paar*
of course!	*natürlich!*
off the coast	*vor der Küste*
off to Brighton	*ab nach Brighton*
off; beef is~	*Rindfleisch ist ausgegangen; schlecht*
off; be ~	*weg sein; aufbrechen*
offer	*Angebot; anbieten*
offer support	*Hilfe anbieten*
old-fashioned	*altmodisch*
omen	*Vorzeichen*
on the run	*auf der Flucht*
once upon a time	*es war einmal*

only eleven o'clock	*erst elf Uhr*
only one pound a seat	*nur ein Pfund pro Platz*
onto; be ~ someone	*jemandem auf den Fersen sein*
operate	*tätig sein; operieren*
operator	*Vermittlung*
opinion	*Meinung*
order	*bestellen; befehlen; Bestellung*
ought; we ~ to be off	*wir sollten aufbrechen*
out-patients; at the ~	*in der Ambulanz*
overdraw one's account	*sein Konto überziehen*
overnight	*über Nacht*
overzealous	*übereifrig*
owe; ~ money	*Geld schulden*
own; on one's ~	*allein*
own; describe in your ~ words	*schildern Sie in Ihren eigenen Worten*
own; owner	*besitzen; Besitzer*

p

p.m.; 2:00 ~ ~	*2 Uhr nachmittags*
pain	*Schmerz*
painful	*schmerzhaft*
parachute	*Fallschirm*
parachuting	*Fallschirmspringen*
parcel	*Päckchen*
part	*Rolle; Teil*
part of	*ein Teil von*
part; be ~ of the service	*zum Service dazugehören*
part; I've done my ~	*ich habe mein Teil getan*
particular; a ~ quality	*eine besondere Eigenschaft*
part-time course	*Halbtagskurs*
pass away	*sterben, verscheiden*
pass each other	*aneinander vorbeifahren*
pass quickly	*schnell vergehen*
pass the quarry	*am Steinbruch vorbeifahren*
pass through one's mind	*durch den Kopf gehen*
passenger door	*Beifahrertür*
passionately; kiss ~	*leidenschaftlich küssen*

patience	*Geduld*
patient	*geduldig; Patient*
pay a visit to	*jemandem einen Besuch abstatten*
pay someone a visit	*jemandem besuchen*
pay up!	*bezahlen Sie!*
payment	*Bezahlung*
peaceful; be ~	*friedlich sein*
peep in	*einen Blick hineinwerfen*
people	*Leute; Volk*
perfectly correct	*vollkommen richtig*
perhaps you're right	*vielleicht hast du Recht*
permanent address	*ständiger Wohnsitz*
permanent guest	*Dauergast*
permanent licence	*Dauergenehmigung*
petrol gauge	*Benzinuhr*
phone the hotel	*das Hotel anrufen*
pick something up	*abholen; aufheben, nehmen*
pick up the phone	*den Hörer abnehmen*
pickle; be in a ~	*in der Klemme sitzen*
piece	*Stück*
piece of paper	*Stück Papier*
pigeon	*Taube*
pile someone into his truck	*jemanden in den Wagen laden*
pile; a ~ of money	*ein Haufen Geld*
place of birth	*Geburtsort*
plane	*Flugzeug*
platform	*Bahnsteig*
pleasant journey	*angenehme Reise*
pleasant-looking	*freundlich aussehend*
pleasure; with ~	*mit Vergnügen*
plenty of time	*viel Zeit*
plot; the ~ thickens	*der Knoten schürzt sich*
pocket	*Tasche, Hosentasche*
point a gun at	*eine Waffe richten auf*
point of view; from his ~ of ~	*aus seiner Sicht*
point; get to the ~	*zur Sache kommen*
poisonous	*giftig*

pool	*Pfütze*
pop up	*auftauchen*
pop up from behind the bar	*hinter der Bar auftauchen*
posh	*piekfein*
possession	*Besitz*
postal code	*Postleitzahl*
potato	*Kartoffel*
pound	*hämmern, klopfen*
pound; his heart was pounding	*sein Herz klopfte*
pour me another	*gieß mir noch einen ein*
powder	*Pulver*
practised	*geübt*
precious; my ~	*kostbar; Schätzchen*
prefer	*vorziehen*
prejudice	*Vorurteil*
preliminary report	*vorläufiger Bericht*
prepare for something	*sich vorbereiten auf etwas*
prescription	*Rezept*
presume something	*etwas annehmen, vermuten*
presumption	*Annahme*
priceless	*kostbar*
prick up one's ears	*die Ohren spitzen*
prime quality	*beste Qualität*
print	*drucken*
print; be in ~	*gedruckt werden*
prison	*Gefängnis*
privately insured	*privat versichert*
probably	*wahrscheinlich*
progress; the meal progressed	*die Mahlzeit nahm ihren Fortgang*
properly	*ordentlich*
property	*Grundstück; Eigentum*
proprietor	*Eigentümer; Besitzer*
prove something	*etwas beweisen*
provide someone with	*jemandem etwas verschaffen*
prying	*neugierig*
psychiatrist	*Psychiater*
pull apart	*aufreißen; auseinander reißen*

pull down the blinds	*die Jalousie herunterlassen*
pull faces (at someone)	*Gesichter schneiden*
pull out	*wegfahren*
pull someone's leg	*sich einen Spaß erlauben mit*
pull something off	*etwas deichseln, schaffen*
pull up	*anhalten (Auto)*
pull up outside the house	*vor dem Haus anhalten*
puncture; I've got a ~	*ich habe einen Platten*
purpose; the ~ of a call	*der Grund eines Anrufs*
purse	*Geldbörse*
push into a room	*sich in ein Zimmer drängen*
push open	*aufstoßen*
push the door	*die Tür aufstoßen*
push; give a car a ~	*ein Auto anschieben*
pushy	*aufdringlich, penetrant*
put someone through	*jemanden (telefonisch) verbinden*
put something at half a million	*etwas auf eine halbe Million schätzen*
put; I don't know how to ~ it	*ich weiß nicht, wie ich es sagen soll*
puzzle something out	*etwas austüfteln*

q

quarry; pass the ~	*am Steinbruch vorbeifahren*
quarter of an hour	*Viertelstunde*
queue	*Warteschlange*
queue up	*sich anstellen*
quietly; do something very ~	*etwas ganz ruhig tun*
quite another thing	*etwas ganz anderes*

r

race; come racing up	*heranrasen*
racing car	*Rennwagen*
racing driver	*Rennfahrer*
radio traffic service	*Straßenverkehrsdienst*
railway station	*Bahnhof*
rain	*regnen; Regen*
rainy day; save money for a ~ ~	*Geld für schlechte Zeiten sparen*
range	*Kollektion*

rapid(ly)	*schnell*
read (read, read)	*lesen*
ready; be ~	*bereit / fertig sein*
realisation	*Erkenntnis; Verwirklichung*
realise	*merken; begreifen; bemerken*
realize; you ~ that...	*das ist euch doch klar, dass ...*
reason	*Grund*
reason to believe	*Grund zur Annahme*
recently	*in letzter Zeit, kürzlich*
reception	*Empfang*
reception desk	*Empfangsschalter*
receptionist	*Empfangsdame, -herr*
reckon	*annehmen*
recognise	*(wieder-)erkennen*
recommend something	*etwas empfehlen*
record something	*etwas schriftlich festhalten*
recover one's health	*wieder gesund werden*
recover something	*etwas wiederbeschaffen*
red-blooded	*vollblütig*
red-skinned	*rothäutig*
refer to something	*sich auf etwas beziehen, auf etwas verweisen; erwähnen*
registration form	*Anmeldungsformular*
Registry of Company Names	*Handelsregister*
regret something	*etwas bereuen; bedauern*
reject something	*etwas ablehnen*
relate something	*etwas erzählen*
relax	*sich entspannen*
relaxation	*Entspannung*
relaxed	*entspannt*
release	*lösen, freigeben*
reliable	*zuverlässig*
remember something	*sich an etwas erinnern*
remember; as you ~	*wie Sie sich erinnern*
remind someone of something	*jemanden an etwas erinnern*
remove something	*etwas entfernen*
rent a car	*ein Auto mieten*

repair shop	*Reparaturwerkstatt*
repay debts	*Schulden zurückzahlen*
repeat	*wiederholen*
reply	*Antwort, antworten*
reply; there was no ~	*keine Antwort*
report to the police	*der Polizei melden*
report; a copy of the ~	*eine Kopie des Berichts*
request	*Bitte; Aufforderung; Anforderung*
request; your ~ is being processed	*Ihr Auftrag wird bearbeitet*
require	*benötigen; brauchen; erfordern*
research	*Nachforschung; Forschung*
reservation	*Reservation*
return ticket	*Rückfahrkarte*
rich	*reich*
rip in two	*in der Mitte zerreißen*
rise, rose, risen	*sich erheben*
risk, take the ~	*das Risiko eingehen*
road accident	*Verkehrsunfall*
robbery	*Raubüberfall*
rocky	*felsig, steinig*
roll over	*sich umdrehen (im Bett)*
round the corner	*um die Ecke*
rubbish	*Unsinn*
rumour	*Gerücht*
rush	*sich beeilen*
rush along	*dahinrasen*
rush on ...	*Ansturm auf ...*
rush upstairs	*nach oben eilen; die Treppe hinaufrennen*

S

safe and sound	*wohlauf, wohlbehalten*
sales twaddle	*Verkaufsgeschwätz*
same; it's the ~	*es ist das Gleiche*
sample; blood ~	*Blutprobe*
satisfy	*zufrieden stellen*
sausage	*Wurst*

save money	*Geld sparen*
save someone's legs	*jemandem den Weg ersparen*
scatter all over the road	*über die ganze Straße verstreuen*
Scot	*Schotte*
scrambling noise	*rascheln*
screech	*quietschen, kreischen*
screen someone	*jemanden überprüfen, durchleuchten*
screw	*Schraube*
screws and bolts	*Schrauben und Bolzen*
sea	*Meer*
search for	*suchen nach*
seat	*Sitz; Sitzplatz*
see from the example of...	*am Beispiel von ... sehen*
seem	*scheinen*
sensible	*vernünftig*
sensitive	*empfindlich/sensibel*
serious	*ernst*
serious; a ~ matter	*eine ernste Angelegenheit*
serve drinks	*Getränke servieren*
set a date	*einen Termin festsetzen*
set off	*aufbrechen; sich aufmachen*
several; for ~ minutes	*mehrere Minuten lang*
sex	*Geschlecht*
shabbily dressed	*schäbig gekleidet*
shape	*Form*
sharp-eyed	*scharfäugig*
shave; that was a close ~	*das hätte ins Auge gehen können*
sheepish; look ~	*dämlich aussehen*
shiver; a cold ~ ran down his back	*ein kalter Schauder lief ihm den Rücken hinunter*
shoes; rather not be in someone's ~.	*nicht in jemandes Haut stecken wollen*
shop assistant	*Verkäufer(in)*
short; money is ~	*Geld ist knapp*
shot	*Schuss*
should; we ~ travel by car	*wir sollten mit dem Auto fahren*
shriek; with its siren shrieking	*mit heulender Sirene*

shuffle	*schlurfen*
sickly	*krank*
sideboard	*Büffet*
sidekick	*Gehilfe*
sigh	*seufzen*
sign	*Verkehrschild*
sign out / check out	*auschecken*
silence	*Stille*
silent; it became ~	*es wurde still*
silly	*dumm; kindisch; albern*
since	*seitdem; da (ja)*
single (room)	*Einzelzimmer*
sink; he felt his heart ~	*das Herz rutschte ihm in die Hose*
sip	*nippen an*
sit across the table	*(jemandem) am Tisch gegenübersitzen*
size	*Größe*
skid	*schleudern (Auto)*
skittles	*Kegeln*
slam the door	*die Tür zuknallen*
slave	*Sklave*
slim cord	*Feinkord*
slip off	*heimlich verschwinden*
slippery	*schlüpfrig; glatt*
slump forward	*nach vorne zusammensacken*
small	*klein*
smarten oneself up	*sich fesch machen*
smash up a car	*ein Auto zu Schrott fahren*
smell	*Geruch; riechen*
smell alcohol	*Alkohol riechen*
smell of	*riechen nach*
smile sweetly	*freundlich lächeln*
snuff out a candle	*eine Kerze ausdrücken*
soft	*sanft*
somehow	*irgendwie*
soon; as ~ as possible	*so bald wie möglich*
sore eyes	*entzündete Augen*
sort	*Sorte, Typ*

sort out	*klären, erledigen*
sort something out	*etwas aufklären*
sound (Adjektiv)	*gesund*
sound good	*sich gut anhören; gut klingen*
soup, be in the ~	*in der Tinte sitzen*
south	*Süden; südlich*
space	*Platz; Zwischenraum*
spare; fit the ~	*den Ersatzreifen montieren*
sparkler	*Klunker*
speak (spoke, spoken)	*sprechen*
speaking of the tea	*da wir gerade vom Tee sprechen*
Speaking	*Am Apparat*
speedometer	*Tachometer*
spell a word	*ein Wort buchstabieren*
spend some time in...	*einige Zeit in ... verbringen*
spend money (spent, spent)	*Geld ausgeben*
spill something	*etwas verschütten*
spill the beans on...	*alles auspacken über ...*
spin	*(sich) drehen*
spin in front of one's eyes	*sich vor jemandes Augen drehen*
spit it out!	*spuck's aus!*
spite; in ~ of	*trotz, ungeachtet*
split second	*Sekundenbruchteil*
spray	*sprühen*
spray someone with something	*jemanden mit etwas besprühen*
spread (spread, spread)	*ausbreiten*
spring in front of the car	*vor das Auto springen*
spring roll	*Frühlingsrolle*
spruce up for a date	*sich für ein Rendezvous schön machen*
staff	*Personal*
stain	*beschmutzen, beflecken*
stairs	*Treppe*
stand (stood, stood)	*stehen; stellen*
stare at	*starren auf*
start off	*aufbrechen*
starting yesterday	*vom gestrigen Tag an*
statement	*Zeugenaussage*

statement of an account	*Kontostand*
stay	*Aufenthalt; bleiben*
stay a whole week	*eine ganze Woche bleiben*
stay with red wine	*beim Rotwein bleiben*
steal (stole, stolen)	*stehlen*
step	*Schritt*
stick insect	*Stabheuschrecke*
stick (stuck stuck); ~ a gun in someone's back	*jemandem eine Pistole in den Rücken drücken*
sticky	*klebrig*
stone's throw; it's only a ~ ~ away.	*es ist nur ein Katzensprung von hier*
stop dead	*erstarrt stehen bleiben*
straight away	*sofort*
strange feelings	*eigenartige Gefühle*
strangely enough	*sonderbarerweise*
string	*Schnur*
stroll around	*herumbummeln*
struggle	*sich abmühen*
stuffed trout	*gefüllte Forelle*
stupid; a ~ situation	*eine dumme Situation*
subject; talk about a ~	*über ein Thema / eine Sache sprechen*
subscriber	*Teilnehmer*
successful(ly)	*erfolgreich*
suddenly	*plötzlich*
suggest something	*etwas vorschlagen*
suit; ~ very well	*gut sitzen (Kleider)*
suit; this car will ~ you	*das Auto wird Ihnen liegen*
summary	*Zusammenfassung*
sun-tanned	*braun gebrannt*
supplier	*Lieferant*
support	*unterstützen / finanzieren*
support; offer ~	*Hilfe anbieten*
suppose she turns up	*angenommen, sie taucht auf*
suppose something	*etwas vermuten, annehmen*
surcharge	*Zuschlag*
sure; I'm not so ~	*ich bin mir nicht so sicher*
surprise	*überraschen*

suspect something	*etwas argwöhnen*
sweat	*schwitzen*
sweaty hands	*verschwitzte Hände*
swig; take a ~ from the bottle	*einen Schluck aus der Flasche nehmen*
swing something open	*etwas aufstoßen*
switch the TV on	*den Fernseher einschalten*
sympathy	*Mitleid*

t

table	*Tisch; Tabelle*
take a deep breath	*tief einatmen*
take someone's name in vain	*über jemanden lästern*
take a room at a hotel	*ein Hotelzimmer nehmen*
take action	*zur Tat schreiten*
take care of a prisoner	*sich um einen Gefangenen kümmern*
take it; I ~ ~ that ...	*ich schließe daraus, dass ...*
take care of	*sich kümmern; sorgen für*
take place	*stattfinden*
take someone seriously	*jemanden ernst nehmen*
take; it ~s over an hour	*man braucht mehr als eine Stunde*
talkative	*gesprächig*
tap the bell	*auf die Klingel tippen*
taste good	*gut schmecken*
teabag	*Teebeutel*
tell (told, told)	*erzählen*
temporary	*vorläufig*
tether; be at the end of one's ~	*nicht mehr weiter wissen*
there's no way around it	*es gibt keine andere Möglichkeit*
thief; thieves (pl)	*Dieb*
think hard	*angestrengt nachdenken*
though	*obwohl; allerdings*
throat	*Kehle*
through train	*durchgehender Zug*
throw a tantrum	*einen Wutanfall bekommen*
throw, threw, thrown	*werfen*
ticket collector	*Schaffner*
ticket counter	*Fahrkartenschalter*

tidy up	*aufräumen*
tie someone up	*jemanden fesseln*
tied up	*verhindert (gefesselt)*
tiptoe into the room	*auf Zehenspitzen in das Zimmer schleichen*
tired	*müde*
tomorrow morning at 6 o'clock	*morgen früh um 6 Uhr*
top of the range model	*Topmodel*
top right-hand corner	*obere rechte Ecke*
tow a car	*ein Auto abschleppen*
towards	*gegen, in Richtung auf*
towards; walk ~ the door	*auf die Tür zugehen*
towel	*Handtuch*
traffic service	*Straßenwacht*
trail	*Spur; Fährte*
trail; lay a false ~	*eine falsche Spur legen*
train; a ~ to Hastings	*ein Zug nach Hastings*
traitor	*Verräter*
transit; in ~	*auf der Durchreise*
transport; I have no ~	*ich habe kein Fahrzeug / Fahrgelegenheit*
travel by car	*mit dem Auto fahren / reisen*
treacherous weed	*verräterisches Kraut*
tricky	*schwierig*
trouble	*Ärger; Umstand; Problem*
trouble; no ~ at all	*überhaupt kein Problem*
trousers; a pair of ~	*Hosen*
truck	*Last-, Lieferwagen*
trust	*trauen; vertrauen; hoffen*
truth; to tell the ~	*um die Wahrheit zu sagen*
tuned	*(hier) geschult*
turn a key in the door	*einen Schlüssel im Schloss drehen*
turn into	*verwandeln in*
turn out to be useful	*sich als nützlich erweisen*
turn up	*auftauchen*
twice	*zweimal*

twitch	*zucken*
tyre print	*Reifenabdruck*

u

umbrella	*Regenschirm*
undercover (investigation)	*verdeckte Ermittlung*
understand)understood, understood)	*verstehen*
unexpected bills	*unerwartete Rechnungen*
unexpected visitors	*unerwartete Besucher*
unless	*es sei denn, wenn nicht*
unlock the door	*die Tür aufsperren*
untidy	*unordentlich*
untie	*aufschnüren*
untie someone	*jemanden losbinden*
until	*bis*
upright; sit ~	*aufrecht sitzen*
upset	*schockiert, durcheinander*
upset be	*aufgeregt sein*
upside, the ~	*das Gute / Positive*
urgent	*dringend*
use something	*etwas gebrauchen, verwenden*
use as a base	*als Ausgangspunkt nutzen*
use one's eyes	*seine Augen aufmachen*
(be) used to; be ~ ~ doing something	*gewohnt sein, etwas zu tun*
useful	*nützlich*

v

vacancy	*freies Zimmer; freie Stelle*
vaccinate against	*impfen gegen*
vain, in ~	*vergebens*
valid documents	*gültige Papiere*
varied	*unterschiedlich, abwechlungsreich*
vehicle	*Fahrzeug*
view	*Sicht*
voice; hear a ~	*eine Stimme hören*

W

waffle	*quasseln, faseln*
waist	*Taille*
waist; get undressed to the ~	*den Oberkörper frei machen*
waiter; waitress	*Kellner; Kellnerin*
walk	*Spaziergang*
ward	*Krankenstation*
warm someone's ear	*jemandem eins hinter die Ohren geben*
warning triangle	*Warndreieck*
waste not, want not	*spare in der Zeit, so hast du in der Not*
waste of a journey	*vergebliche Reise*
waste of time	*Zeitverschwendung*
waste; what a ~!	*was für eine Verschwendung!*
way; not know which ~ to turn	*weder aus noch ein wissen*
ways; change one's ~	*seine Gewohnheiten ändern*
wear (wore, worn); be wearing something	*etwas anhaben; tragen*
weary, wearily	*müde*
weather	*Wetter*
weed	*Unkraut*
week	*Woche*
weightlifter	*Gewichtheber*
wellness	*Wohlbefinden*
well-to-do; a ~ gentlemen	*ein wohlhabender Herr*
what about ...?	*wie steht es mit ...; wie wär's mit ...?*
what the hell ...	*was zum Teufel ...*
what was it all about?	*um was ging es?*
while	*während*
whirlwind	*Wirbelwind*
who	*wer; der, die*
who else?	*wer / wen sonst?*
whole; a ~ week	*eine ganze Woche*
whole; the ~ thing	*die ganze Sache*
wide; a ~ road	*eine breite Straße*
wind down the window	*das Fenster herunterkurbeln*
withdraw money	*Geld abheben*
word; be as good as one's ~	*zu seinem Wort stehen*
work wonders	*Wunder wirken*

workmanship	*Handwerk (-skunst)*
worried	*besorgt*
worry	*sich Sorgen machen*
worse	*schlimmer*
worth, be ~ it	*sich lohnen*
worth; be ~ a lot	*viel wert sein*
worth; it is ~ learning	*es lohnt sich, es zu lernen*
write a protocol (wrote, written)	*ein Protokoll aufnehmen*

x, y

X-ray	*Röntgenaufnahme*
yawn	*gähnen*

rororo
© Britta Lembke

Robert Kleinschroth
Anne-Laure Maupai | Dieter Maupai
FRANZÖSISCH
FÜR BÜFFELMUFFEL
rororo

Dieter Nuhr
Gibt es intelligentes Leben?

Fassungslos steht Dieter Nuhr vor dem großen kosmischen Durcheinander des menschlichen Daseins und fragt sich: «Gibt es intelligentes Leben?» An 15 abgelegenen Orten versucht er, eine Antwort zu finden – pointiert, bissig, satirisch.
rororo 62076

Comedians bei rororo: Gibt es bessere Unterhaltung?

Wigald Boning
Bekenntnisse eines Nachtsportlers

Auf seine unverwechselbare Art erzählt Wigald Boning von seinen skurrilen Trainingserlebnissen und ungewöhnlichen Trainingsmethoden, versieht das Ganze mit Tipps für Sportler und Möchtegern-Sportler und bietet vor allem eins: Amüsement.
rororo 62192

Bernhard Hoëcker
Aufzeichnungen eines Schnitzeljägers
Mit Gëocaching zurück zur Natur

Jede freie Minute begibt sich Bernhard Hoëcker auf Schatzsuche. Mit viel Humor erzählt er von seinen außergewöhnlichen Abenteuern und erklärt alles, was man über Geocaching wissen muss.
rororo 62252

S 79/1

Weitere Informationen in der Rowohlt Revue *oder unter* www.rororo.de